WINDOWS OF THE SOUL

Stained Glass of the Church of the Most Holy Trinity
AUGUSTA, GEORGIA

by

GAIL DUFFIE STEBBINS

Iconographic Descriptions and History
by
DEBORAH S. JAMIESON, Ph.D.

Best Wishes /
Deborah Jamie—

Photographed
by
**ED BELINSKI/TALKING HORSE MEDIA,
DEBORAH S. JAMIESON,
AND MARY ELEANOR STEBBINS**

Published for the Bicentennial Celebration of
the Church of the Most Holy Trinity
Augusta, Georgia
2010

All history and iconography sections are the work of Deborah S. Jamieson, Ph.D., Assistant Professor, Art History, Armstrong Atlantic State University, Savannah, Georgia. She also provided the photography for all window details. All photos enhanced in PhotoShop by David Warren, a graphic design student at Armstrong Atlantic State University.

Photographs of all Franz Mayer and Company windows in the book appear courtesy of Ed Belinski/Talking Horse Media, Augusta, Georgia.

Photographs of the G.C. Riordan windows in the apse and the Franz Mayer and Company photographs on the cover appear courtesy of Mary Eleanor Stebbins, an independent lighting designer in Boston, Massachusetts.

Gail Duffie Stebbins acted as editor as well as co-author with Dr. Jamieson, and selected the traditional prayers and meditations included in the book.

ISBN 978-1-4507-3618-3

Printed in Augusta, Georgia by Strother's Printing, Inc.

EDITOR'S PREFACE

In August, 2009, the Chairman of the Bicentennial Committee, Maura Jabaley, asked me to consider working on a book to honor the parish's 200 year anniversary. I said, "yes," and began praying for inspiration. Windows of the Soul is the result. It seems so obvious to me now, but at the start of the journey, I had no idea what type of book would result.

A call to Father Allan McDonald, who oversaw the restoration of the church in the late 1990's, focused my attention on the windows. It was not that I had overlooked them. Those windows have always transported me into the presence of God. All fifteen of those large windows are my dear friends (even though I must confess that the Annunciation window is my particular favorite).

In talking about the history of the church with Father Allan, I realized the possibility of highlighting those magnificent windows. The twelve along the side were made by Franz Mayer and Company and placed in the church in the early twentieth century. The three behind the altar are of a different provenance and time, going back to the nineteenth century. What a wonderful way to tie together our history!

My search for information about the windows led me to Dr. Deborah S. Jamieson, assistant professor of art at Armstrong Atlantic State University in Savannah, Georgia, who just happens to be an expert on stained glass art and particularly on the Franz Mayer and Company stained glass windows. I extend my sincere and heartfelt thanks to Dr. Jamieson for graciously agreeing to be part of this book and for her fruitful research into the history of those front three windows.

Thank you, Ed Belinski, for volunteering your time and great talent to be the photographer for the project. You made the book a reality.

DEDICATION

"And how can they believe in him of whom they have not heard? And how can they hear without someone to preach? And how can people preach unless they are sent?" (Romans 10:14,15).

This book is dedicated to the courageous men who have served, are serving, and will serve in the parish of the Church of the Most Holy Trinity, in Augusta, Georgia. We thank the Lord for these men who have eagerly embraced the cross of Jesus. Simon the Cyrenian shouldered the cross only when drafted into service by the Roman soldiers (Matthew 27:32). Daily, our priests reach out for the cross, grasping it with willing hearts and hands.

We know their service is not easy. Their path is not smooth. Jesus is said to have fallen three times on his way to Calvary. Each time, he lifted himself up on hands and knees to rise again, knowing that our salvation depended upon his reaching Golgotha and being crucified upon the cross. Satan undoubtedly encouraged Jesus to give up on the road and not to finish his work. Jesus' love for his Father and for us gave him the strength to persevere, until he could cry out in his agony on the cross, "It is finished" (John 19:30).

As we reflect on the ultimate life-giving sacrifice of Jesus, so too we think on the work facing a priest, who stands with the flock as protector against the forces of Darkness. "For our struggle is not with flesh and blood but with the principalities, with the powers, with the world rulers of this present darkness, with the evil spirits in the heavens" (Ephesians 6:12). And standing before, beside and behind the priest [and us] at all times is the power of the Lord, God Almighty. A parish priest's task is nothing less than to bring faith to unbelievers, to convert sinners, to give fervor to the lukewarm, to stimulate the good to become even better, and to help the holy walk at the highest level.

"How beautiful are the feet of those who bring good news!"

TABLE OF CONTENTS

INTRODUCTION

In 1850, the Diocese of Savannah was created by Pope Pius IX. By that time, the Catholic community in Augusta had been celebrating Mass in its first church building for 28 years and was already raising funds to build a larger church.

This book is centered on the 15 large stained glass windows of that "larger church" --the Church of the Most Holy Trinity in Augusta, Georgia. This church is one of the two oldest Catholic Church buildings in Georgia. Its predecessor of the same name was the first Catholic Church built in Georgia.

Although the earliest Catholic presence in the area now known as the State of Georgia dates from the 16th century when Franciscans established a network of mission stations, these missions had limited success. Subsequently, in the 18th century when the British assumed control of the area, Catholicism was banned. It was only after the Revolutionary War that Catholics were granted the right to practice their faith within the state in recognition of the service of nearly 3,900 French, Haitian, and Irish Catholic troops at the Siege of Savannah in 1779.

According to records in existence in 1914, the first recorded Catholic Mass in Augusta was celebrated by Abbe Carnele, from Savannah, in 1798. Beginning in 1800, regular services were held in Augusta. In 1810 the Rev. Robert Browne, O.S.A., was sent to Augusta by the Bishop of Baltimore to buy land and begin erection of a small church. A charter of incorporation was obtained from the General Assembly and the church was dedicated on Christmas Day, 1812.

In 1820, eight years after this church was built in Augusta, the Diocese of Charleston was created. The state of Georgia and both Carolinas were part of the diocese. In 1850, when there were approximately 5,000 Catholics within Georgia, the Diocese of Savannah was created by Pope Pius IX.

Seven years before the creation of the Savannah diocese, the Church of the Most Holy Trinity congregation had outgrown the original church. The first building was initially enlarged, but in 1853 the decision was made that a new building was needed. The collection of funds for construction of the new church was interrupted temporarily by the yellow fever epidemic of 1854. The cornerstone was laid July 19,1857.

The plans and drawings for the church were donated by John Rudolph Niersee, head architect for the Baltimore & Ohio Railroad. He also designed the South Carolina State House. Construction slowly proceeded on the new church. When funds ran low, the work stopped until more money was raised. Parishioners volunteered their time and skills to work on the project.

The War Between the States caused further delays. The blockade, set up by the Northern Army, prevented the delivery of building materials and stopped artisans from entering the state. Baltimore artist John Mullen ran the blockade to complete the three marble altars in the church. The Jardine organ was too large to be smuggled through the blockade and did not arrive until after the consecration of the church on April 12, 1863.

Both the new church and the one it replaced were consecrated under the title and name of the Church of the Holy Trinity. By 1914, it was well known as St. Patrick's because of its primary patron saint. When the downtown Augusta churches merged in 1971, the Church was again called by its original name, expanded slightly, to be the Church of the Most Holy Trinity.

Two different studios created the windows featured in this book. The provenance of the twelve side windows has never been a mystery. These windows, which depict scenes from the lives of Mary and of Our Lord Jesus Christ, were designed by Franz Mayer and Company of Munich, Germany in 1919. Dr. Jamieson has now identified the source of the three large windows illuminating the apse: G.C. Riordan & Company.

PASTORAL REFLECTIONS

A number of the priests who have served at the Church of the Most Holy Trinity agreed to share their thoughts about the stained glass windows of the church. I offer you their words.

Msgr. O'Neill

Of those priests, the oldest serving priest in the diocese is the Rev. Msgr. William O. O'Neill, V.G., Rector of the Cathedral of St. John the Baptist in Savannah, Georgia. Msgr. O'Neill was ordained in 1967. He served at the Church of the Most Holy Trinity from 1971 to 1975, when the three downtown parishes of Immaculate Conception, Sacred Heart, and St. Patrick's were merged. Prior to that he was Associate Pastor at Immaculate Conception in Augusta from 1968 to 1971.

Msgr. O'Neill, in recalling his service in Augusta, declares that all of the windows at the Church of the Most Holy Trinity are special to him, although he is 'somewhat partial' to the center apse window depicting the Holy Trinity after which the church is named. Although the parish was known unofficially as St. Patrick's after its favorite patron saint during much of its history, its official name has always been that of Most Holy Trinity.

Msgr. Costigan

The Rev. Msgr. P. James Costigan, V.F., ordained in 1968, served the church from 1971 to 1972. His favorite window is that of Jesus teaching the children. As Msgr. Costigan notes, children had a very special place in Jesus' heart. Jesus himself told the people, "Let the children come to me; do not hinder them." At another point he set the children up as examples of the Kingdom – "unless you become like little children you cannot enter the kingdom of God." Throughout his ministry on earth Jesus showed a great tenderness and love of these "little ones."

Fr. McDonald

The Rev. Allan J. McDonald, ordained in 1980, served as Pastor from 1991 to 2004. He oversaw the renovation of the church that restored it to its full beauty. "To ask me which is my favorite window in the Church of the Most Holy Trinity is like asking a child which is his favorite M&M, all of them!"

Nevertheless, he is partial to the window of the Resurrection of Our Lord. He recalls looking at all of the windows since he worked at the now closed Davison's Department Store in the early 1970's in downtown Augusta. He would attend daily Mass during his lunch hour and usually the Vigil Mass on Saturday after work. He would marvel at all of the windows, but was always intrigued by the Resurrection window which shows Christ in His power and glory after the resurrection, coming forth triumphant from the tomb, with the soldiers awestruck in fear and trepidation even to the point of covering their heads. Jesus holds in His raised hand the banner of victory, not just for the triumph of His power over sin and death, but for our triumph in Him as well.

All of the windows are like the various facets of a fine diamond. They sparkle, tantalizing the eyes in a hypnotic way, but also illuminating the soul not with hypnosis, but with vigorous clarity. These are windows into the human and divine which intersect and become One in Christ Jesus. These windows instruct, inspire and motivate us to be authentic followers of Jesus, trusting in His power to save us unto life everlasting. The Resurrection is like the "big bang theory." It is the source and summit of our faith, hope and love that are gifts from God that enable us to know, love and serve Jesus Christ, crucified and risen and Who is "the way, the truth and the life."

Fr. McDonald also has a second favorite window: the Nativity, but not for its beauty. Of all of the windows it has the least detail and color. It exists today because of a miracle that occurred during the restoration process. When Conrad Schmitt and

Company who restored the Church and the three windows above the altar removed the Nativity window, it was in such disrepair that when they walked it out of the church in one piece and exited the front doors by the wheelchair ramp, one of the large middle sections of the window fell out.

By a miracle of God, a parishioner walking up the ramp to enter the church happened to be there at that precise moment and caught the falling segment before it hit the ground where it would have exploded into a thousand splintered, glistening fragments that like Humpty Dumpty could never have been put back together by all the King's men. The Most Holy Trinity and good old Saint Patrick, one of the church's patron saints along with Saint Vincent de Paul, were like the soldiers guarding the tomb of Jesus, but now protecting the precious cargo being sent for restoration.

The restored windows are a constant reminder that all of us are in need of restoration. We do not need a firm that specializes in such to do it for us. We need Jesus Christ who alone can accomplish what is needed for the sin sick soul. These windows remind us that the Church is not a hotel for saints, but a refuge fro sinners in need of redemption, clergy and laity alike. In this sense the church building is like a spa in an art gallery. It restores us to complete health while inspiring us with God's beauty in the process.

Fr. Lubinsky

The Rev. Michael Lubinsky, ordained in 1978, has served the Church as Parochial Vicar since 2001 and briefly served as Interim Pastor in 2009. Father Lubinsky's favorite window is that of Saint Margaret Mary Alacoque witnessing the Sacred Heart of Jesus in her devotions. The knowledge that saints of years ago have given their whole lives for the mystical truth of Jesus being our Saviour and Lord and have had actual visions of Christ with His heart open to our eyes to see His depth of holy love is amazing and beautiful, emotionally moving to the core of our souls. What happiness to see that before we get to heaven, the Lord is sharing with us visions of His own Sacred Heart opened up for us to see the depth of His care for us. This stained glass window opens to us the vision of how much Jesus loves us and the whole wide world with a heart of much love and mercy. He extends it to us richly.

Fr. Brannen

The Rev. Brett A. Brannen, ordained in 1991, was Pastor during 2004 and 2005. Fr. Brannen loves best the window of the death of Saint Joseph. The Catholic Church has always revered Saint Joseph under many titles: the foster father of Jesus, the Guardian of the Redeemer, the patron saint of fathers, the patron saint of workers, the patron saint of carpenters and the patron saint of the universal Church. But there is another concept often associated with this gentle, holy man. Saint Joseph is the patron saint of a happy death.

Although the death of Saint Joseph is not mentioned in Sacred Scripture, obviously we know it happened. We do not know how or when Saint Joseph died – only that he is never mentioned again after the finding of the child Jesus in the temple (Luke 2:41-52). And he is not quoted as saying any words in that passage. Christian tradition also represents Mary as a widow during the adult ministry of Jesus (Jn 19:26-27). Therefore, the tradition to revere Saint Joseph as the patron saint of a happy death developed in the Catholic Church because it is assumed that he died in the arms of Jesus and Mary (or at least in their presence). The stained glass window illustrates this scene beautifully.

"Our love is brought to perfection in this, that we should have confidence on the Day of Judgment...Love has no room for fear. Perfect love casts out all fear..." (1 Jn $:17-17). Let us pray that Jesus will perfect our love and teach us how to love the way everyone loves in heaven.

Many people still fear death. As we look at the stained glass window of Saint Joseph, may we pray for a happy death for ourselves: to die without fear...in the arms of Jesus and Mary. Saint Joseph, pray for us!

Fr. Donahue

The Rev Timothy C. Donahue, ordained in 2000, served as Pastor during the years 2005 through 2009. Fr. Donahue recalls first visiting the Church of the Most Holy Trinity while he was a seminarian in the early 1990's and being overwhelmed by the majesty and solemnity of the holy space.

Fr. Donahue's favorite window is the image of Saint Bernadette praying to the Blessed Mother in the Grotto of Lourdes. From the presider's chair, this was the window he gazed upon most intently during the course of the Mass. The knowledge that Mary was always there at the celebration of her Son in the Eucharist was always a source of great comfort and peace.

The theology informing the stained glass windows is perfectly consistent with the twin sources of revelation for the Faith: Scripture and Tradition. Each window tells a story and symbolizes the march of the Catholic pilgrimage over the ages.

Not only do the stained glass windows of the church enshrine for us the stories and chapters of our faith, but they also symbolize to us the life of a Christian. The windows only reflect the story of Christ when light is shining through them. For this reason we cannot determine an image on the stained glass from outside the church. This mirrors our lives as Christians: without the light of Christ shining through us, we cannot tell the story of our faith.

Fr. Kavanaugh

The Rev. Michael J. Kavanaugh, ordained in 1985, began serving as Pastor in the parish in 2009. Fr. Kavanaugh recalls that the first Mass he celebrated at the church was a mass for the students of Immaculate Conception School. He had just been transferred from Our Lady of Lourdes parish in Port Wentworth, Georgia. Sitting in the presider's chair and looking upon the splendor of the Mayer window which was the image of Our Lady of Lourdes as she appeared to Saint Bernadette gave him a sense of continuity and belonging.

In all of her appearances, Our Lady has been made manifest to the poor, the suffering, the "simple" people who are in need of consolation. In Vietnam the Blessed Virgin appeared at LaVang in 1798 to members of the Catholic community who were being hunted down in an anti-Catholic pogrom started by King Cahn 'Minh. In Cuba around 1600, Our Lady of Charity was revealed to two native Indians and a ten year old slave boy whose canoe was being tossed about in a storm. Her presence has always been offered as a sign of hope, a sign of consolation.

Since the time that Mary appeared to the poor shepherd girl, Bernadette Soubirous, Lourdes has been a place of healing, with thousands of pilgrims visiting each year to bathe in the waters that flow from a spring that Saint Bernadette found after digging in the ground. Looking closely at the image in the glass, one can see a number of wild red roses growing in the rocks, but the roses that have touched Mary's feet have become gold in color.

Through Mary's intercession, may we continue to grow closer to her Son, and by the way we live our lives, may we continue to proclaim to all we meet the saving mystery of His life, death and resurrection.

Detail of G.C. Riordan & Company studio signature

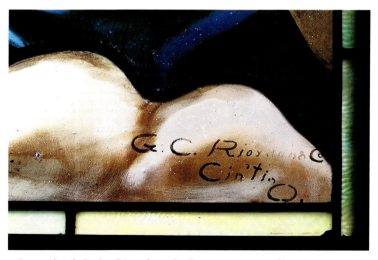

Detail of G.C. Riordan & Company studio signature

Detail of Franz Mayer and Company studio signature

Detail of Franz Mayer and Company studio signature

The Art of Stained Glass

Stained glass is a dynamic art form whose colors continually shift, adjusting to the intensity of light throughout the day and over the passing of the seasons. While serving the practical function of a light source for interior architectural spaces as well as a source of aesthetic and spiritual appeal, stained glass is an artistic expression whose beginnings date to the ancient world.

The ancient Romans used glass in windows as well as other translucent materials and arranged them into patterned window frames of wood, plaster or bronze, a technique widely practiced throughout the Roman world. Although no complete windows from the sixth century or earlier have survived, an abundance of literary evidence testifies to the early use of colored pieces of glass in the windows of churches. The writings of Prudentius (348-c.410), St Augustine of Hippo (354-386), St Sidonius Apollinaris (c. 324-480) and St Gregory of Tours (538-594) give vivid descriptions of the colored glass windows located in the various churches they encountered.

We can look to the histories of St Gregory and the Venerable Bede (673-735) to see what a momentous role the Church played in preserving the cultural and artistic achievements of the Romans, including the glazing of glass, after the collapse of the Empire. According to Bede, Abbot Benedict Biscop (628-690) sent for craftsmen to make and glaze the windows of his monastery church at Monkwearmouth in Northumbria, thus reviving the lost art of glazing windows in England.

It is not known when paint was first applied and fired onto window glass, an important characteristic of most stained glass, but fragments of painted glass date to as early as about 540. The earliest surviving complete figures in painted stained glass are four figures of prophets in the Augsburg Cathedral that date to c. 1100. Because of the sophisticated rendering of the figures it is assumed that there was already a well established artistic and technical tradition of glass painting.

Stained glass emerged as a prominent feature of Christian architecture through a landmark event during the 1140s, the rebuilding of the choir of Saint-Denis by the powerful and influential patron, Abbot Suger (1081-1151). Never had stained glass been used on this scale before; the choir walls literally became luminous and radiant walls of glass. Perhaps more than anyone else, Suger was responsible for establishing the stained glass window as a prominent feature of Christian architecture. In the century following the completion of Saint-Denis monumental stained glass windows became a central element of Gothic architecture in France and throughout Europe.

Suger's writings reflect his concern for the symbolic and spiritual qualities of color, light, and brilliance, all traits of the medium of stained glass. He believed that by contemplating the windows, one might come closer to God. Light and color were a means by which he could redirect his thoughts from the temporal world to the spiritual world of divine virtues, a means by which his soul could be illuminated and united with God.

The Gothic style dominated stained glass in Europe between the thirteenth and fifteenth centuries. The accelerated rise in population and urban cities was accompanied by a flourishing in construction of the great cathedrals, monumental structures filled with elaborate and magnificent programs of painted glass. Stained glass windows quickly became the dominant mode of Christian pictorial narrative during the medieval period.

During the sixteenth century a rapid decline began in the production as well as the quality of stained glass that continued over the next several centuries. Colored glass was difficult to find and technical knowledge was forgotten and lost. However, by the end of the nineteenth century stained glass had regained an important place among the arts.

The Gothic Revival in nineteenth century Europe created an unprecedented demand for stained glass. A Bavarian resurgence in glass making emerged under the patronage of King Ludwig I (1825-48). Ludwig began state-sponsored experimentation in the production of colored glass in Munich in 1824 which quickly led to his founding of the Königliche Glasmalereianstalt, or the Royal Bavarian Glass Painting Institute. Out of this rich artistic revival in Munich emerged a number of prosperous and successful German stained glass studios that, following the aesthetic traditions promoted by the Royal Bavarian Glass Painting Institute, forged the distinctive Munich style.

The Munich Style favored naturalism and looked to traditional easel painting for inspiration. Skilled glaziers incorporated perspective designs that transformed decorative two-dimensional stained glass into illusionist works of art. Placed within clearly defined three-dimensional spaces, large and idealized figural types are displayed with brilliant color, precise linear contouring and great clarity of design. Harmonious and symmetrical figural groupings are depicted with a directness and realism that encourages emotional participation with the sacred narratives. Such stylistic characteristics, coupled with the complete familiarity Munich artists had with Catholic pictorial traditions and iconography, resulted in the Munich style becoming the definitive Catholic style by the close of the century.

The Stained Glass Collection at Most Holy Trinity

The Munich style is superbly demonstrated in the stained glass collection at Most Holy Trinity Church. The church boasts original sets of figural stained glass produced by two highly successful stained glass studios, G.C. Riordan & Company and Franz Mayer and Company. Both companies were founded around the mid-nineteenth century and by the end of the century had risen to national prominence. Significant examples of their work can be found in numerous churches and cathedrals across the United States — spectacular pictures in glass whose quality craftsmanship and timeless beauty continue to delight and inspire.

G.C. Riordan & Company

The three large chancel windows date to the 1890s and were crafted by G.C. Riordan & Company, an American studio that emerged in Cincinnati, Ohio. Prior to this publication, neither the identity of the studio nor an approximate date of construction was known for the three large chancel windows. After extensive research and looking to noted specialists in stained glass for assistance the studio identified. The windows date to the 1890s and were crafted by G.C. Riordan & Company, an American studio that emerged in Cincinnati, Ohio. The original founders of the Riordan Company were William Coulter from Ireland and Joseph Finagin from Maryland, and the studio is described as the oldest documented continuously operated stained glass studio in the United States. Coulter and Finagin opened their studio in 1838 near the banks of the Ohio River and are listed in the 1840 city directory as glass cutters. Coulter soon became the sole proprietor and it was after his son John joined the studio that it became known as William Coulter & Son.

Although the firm was the earliest Cincinnati establishment dealing in decorative glass, the art of glass painting appears to have been introduced into the area by other craftsmen. However, the studio of William & Coulter continued to quickly expand their areas of expertise as is demonstrated by their listing in the 1876-75 city directory as glass painters.

Gerald C. Riordan of Limerick County, Ireland, managed the studio from 1884-1892. The company's name changed when purchased by Gerald in 1892 and was advertised as G.D. Riordan & Company the following year. Under his leadership Riordan & Company continued to enlarge its services and work toward developing a national reputation. A pivotal event in the growth of the company was the joining of Gerald's brother, John as co-founder in 1894. Together the Riordan brothers greatly increased the number of commissions that were coming from throughout the United States and by the late 1800s, the studio of G.C. Riordan & Company was on its way to national prominence.

In the Cincinnati area and across the country the popular Munich style was highly fashionable during the nineteenth and into the twentieth century. G.C. Riordan & Company favored the Munich style and embraced Renaissance pictorial traditions as reflected in the three chancel windows at Most Holy Trinity. A stylistic characteristic particular to the Riordan studio is the heavy application of colored glass enamels onto large pieces of glass for heightened naturalism. The framing of the windows with expansive, opulent borders composed of highly textured and multi-colored pieces of opalescent glass are also characteristic of their work. The decorative borders of the Riordan windows reflect Aesthetic designs that were highly popular with American artists during the last years of the nineteenth century.

In 1975, the studio's ownership passed to an Austrian immigrant, Walter Bambach. Bambach trained as a glass painter in Austria at the monastery of Kloster Schlierbach, an important European center still today for the study of glass and glass painting. The Riordan studio sent for him in 1955, and he later bought the studio after John Riordan retired. Under Bambauch's direction the firm was relocated across the Ohio River from Cincinnati to Covington, Kentucky.

Since 2002 the studio has been owned and operated by stained glass artisans Jay and Linda Moorman and is currently located in Middletown, Ohio. Renamed the Beauverre-Riordan Stained Glass Studio, Jay and Linda are continuing to uphold the company's long established reputation in the production of American stained glass.

Franz Mayer'sche Hofkunstanstalt

Franz Mayer and Company of Munich

The twelve figural windows distributed along the side nave walls were produced by Franz Mayer and Company of Munich, Germany, and date to around 1920. The Mayer studio signature can be found in the lower right area of four windows: Mary of Lourdes; The Flight into Egypt; The Wedding at Cana; and The Death of Joseph.

The Mayer Company has continuously operated as a family firm since its founding in 1847 by Josef Gabriel Mayer. Today the managing partners of the company are Josef's grandson Gabriel, and Gabriel's son Michael. Originally specializing in the manufacture of ecclesiastical furnishings, in 1863 the company expanded into the production of stained glass and growth came quickly. In 1865 a branch of the company was founded in London, followed by another in Dublin and one in New York in 1888. It was only a mere half a century earlier that Joseph Gabriel Mayer began what was to be a legendary and extremely profitable career in the field of stained glass.

The American populace highly favored their stained glass for by the end of the century 90% of the windows made by Franz Mayer and Company were being exported to the United States. Their popularity and reputation in the field of stained glass and liturgical furnishing was greatly enhanced through numerous prestigious titles and commissions. Ludwig II, King of Bavaria and the grandson of Ludwig I, awarded the firm in 1882 the title "Royal Bavarian Court Institution." Pope Leo XIII bestowed the title "Pontifical Institute of Christian Art" ten years later. In the early 1900s Pope Pius X commissioned the large Holy Spirit stained glass window located above the Cathedra Petri, or the Throne of St. Peter, in St. Peter's Basilica in Rome. Being the only stained glass window ever installed in St. Peter's and, not withstanding its coveted location behind Bernini's high altar, is testimony to the Church's sanction and approval of the firm's product.

The Mayer designers were completely familiar with the pictorial traditions of their audiences, such as depictions of the Sacraments, the Mysteries of the Rosary, or favorite saints of ethnic popularity. Mindful of the writings of Pope Gregory the Great who encouraged the use of images in devotion to show 'the invisible by means of the visible,' a long pictorial tradition exists with the Church of using images to draw the worshipper emotionally closer to the divine. The Mayer artists functioned as successors to this great tradition and were exceptionally gifted in executing illusionist depictions of biblical stories imbued with spiritual and devotional significance. Their dramatic window scenes still succeed in drawing the viewer in, encouraging a quiet and concentrated contemplation of the Christian faith.

The current studio of Franz Mayer and Company was built in 1922/23 by renowned architect Theodor Fischer and is considered a historical landmark in downtown Munich. While a respected leader today in the production and conservation of stained glass and mosaic, the studio also services and facilitates on-site collaborations with independent artists, designers and architects.

THE HOLY TRINITY

"We do not confess three Gods, but one God in three persons, the 'consubstantial Trinity.' The divine persons do not share the one divinity among themselves but each of them is God whole and entire: 'The Father is that which the Son is, the Son that which the Father is, the Father and the Son that which the Holy Spirit is, i.e.; by nature one God'"
Catechism Of the Catholic Church (253)

The Father is God (Exodus 3:14), Jesus is God (John 8:58), and the Holy Spirit is God (Acts 5:3-4), but there is only one God (Deuteronomy 6:4; James 2:19). How these two statements of doctrine can both be true is the mystery of the Trinity.

All three Persons are fully God. They are identical in attributes and equal in power, mercy, justice, holiness, knowledge and all other qualities. No Person of the Trinity is inferior to another, each Person of the Trinity is distinct from the others, and when speaking of the Trinity as a whole, one speaks of no greater being than the Father, the Son, or the Holy Spirit alone. Just as God has always existed, there was never a time when one of the Persons of the Godhead did not exist. They are all eternal.

The Church teaches that the mystery of the Trinity is the revelation regarding God's nature which Jesus Christ, the Son of God, came upon earth to deliver to the world and the foundation of the Church's entire dogmatic system. The central doctrine of the Christian religion is the truth that in the unity of the Godhead there are Three Persons, the Father, the Son, and the Holy Spirit, these Three Persons being truly distinct one from another.

The Trinity is the perfect model for us of selfless love. God is defined as Love. Within His own being, the Love unites, gives, and shares perfectly within the Godhead. And yet, while perfectly selfless in their mutual sharing of the divine nature, the Persons in the Trinity do not cease to be themselves.

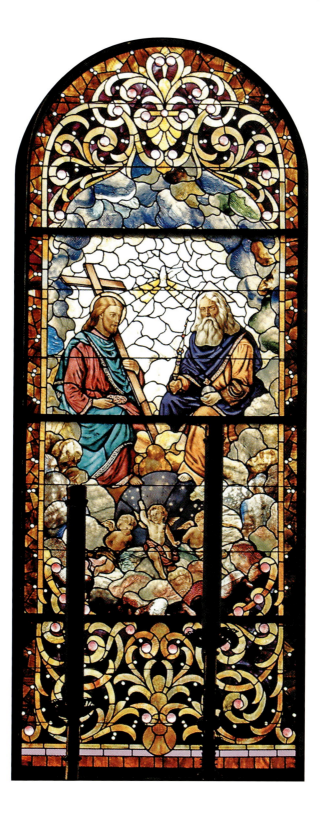

THE HOLY TRINITY ICONOGRAPHY

The mystery of the Most Holy Trinity has from the earliest times been taught by the Catholic Church and is the central doctrine of Christian faith and life. God alone can make it known to us by revealing himself as Father, Son, and Holy Spirit. This doctrine was defined at the First Ecumenical Council at Nicea (325) and confirmed at the Council of Constantinople (381). The truth that in the unity of the Godhead there are Three Persons, the Father, the Son, and the Holy Spirit, is expressed in the baptismal commission given by Jesus to His apostles: "Go therefore and make disciples of all nations, baptizing them in the name of the Father and of the Son and of the Holy Spirit" (Matthew 28:19).

This namesake window of the Church of the Most Holy Trinity is centrally located in the apse, directly above and behind the high altar. Its prominent placement makes the image the visual focus of the church, speaks to its significance within the entire program of windows, and underlines the fundamental theological importance of this dogma.

Enthroned in the heavens and suspended amid multi-colored, billowing clouds, God the Father and Christ are central to the composition, their bodies turned inward while sitting side by side. Their feet rest on a dark blue globe sprinkled with gold stars, which serves as a royal footstool. The globe representing the planet Earth and man's physical realm, is linked to the heavenly throne.

Supporting the sphere is a trio of winged cherubim whose wings are spread upward. The inclusion of these angels is intended to recall those that flanked the Ark of the Covenant, the symbolic throne of God.

The depiction of God the Father is based upon Daniel's vision of the Ancient of Days (Daniel 7:9) which became the artistic convention — an old man with white hair and a long beard. His right hand holds a jeweled scepter, an age-old symbol of sovereignty and authority. In His left rests an orb surmounted by a cross, associated with sovereignty and more specifically the triumph of Christ and His Church over the world. Another distinctive attribute of God the Father is the equilateral triangular nimbus placed behind His head. This halo is distinctive to God the Father and is said to refer also to the Holy Trinity.

Following traditional depictions, the Son is seated at the right hand of the Father and is depicted as a younger man. Wearing a red gown reminiscent of His martyrdom, He carries two symbols of His Passion, a Cross and a Crown of Thorns.

A white dove, symbolizing the Holy Spirit (John 1:32) is symmetrically placed between the Father and the Son, hovering with extended wings. Diagonal rays of golden light emanate outward from the dove and extend to the two figures, a symbolic representation of the unity of three distinct persons: the Father, Son, and Holy Spirit, the consubstantial Trinity.

THE BREASTPLATE OF SAINT PATRICK

I bind unto myself today the strong name of the Trinity,
By invocation of the same, the Three in One and One in Three.

I bind this day to me forever, by power of faith, Christ's
Incarnation; His baptism in the Jordan River; His death on
cross for my salvation; His bursting from the spiced tomb;
His riding up the heavenly way; His coming at the day of
doom; I bind unto myself today.

I bind unto myself the power of the great love of the Cherubim;
the sweet "Well done" in judgment hour; the service
of the Seraphim, Confessors' faith, Apostles' word,
the Patriarchs' prayers, the Prophets' scrolls,
all good deeds done unto the Lord, and purity of virgin souls.

I bind unto myself today the virtues of the starlit heaven,
the glorious sun's life-giving ray, the whiteness of the moon
at even, the flashing of the lightning free, the whirling
wind's tempestuous shocks, the stable earth, the deep
salt sea, around the old eternal rocks.

I bind unto myself today the power of God to hold and lead,
His eye to watch, His might to stay, His ear to hearken to my
need; the wisdom of my God to teach, His hand to guide,
His shield to ward, the word of God to give me speech,
His heavenly host to be my guard.

Against the demon snares of sin, the vice that gives
temptation force, the natural lusts that war within, the hostile
men that mar my course; or few or many, far or nigh, in every
place and in all hours against their fierce hostility, I bind to me
these holy powers. Against all Satan's spells and wiles, against
false words of heresy, against the knowledge that defiles, against
the heart's idolatry, against the wizard's evil craft, against the
death-wound and the burning, the choking wave and the poisoned
shaft, protect me, Christ, till Thy returning.

Christ be with me, Christ within me, Christ behind me,
Christ before me, Christ beside me, Christ to win me,

Christ to comfort and restore me, Christ beneath me,
Christ above me, Christ in quiet, Christ in danger,
Christ in hearts of all that love me, Christ in
mouth of friend and stranger.

I bind unto myself the name, the strong name of the
Trinity; by invocation of the same, the Three in One, and
One in Three, of whom all nature hath creation,
Eternal Father, Spirit, Word: praise to the Lord of
my salvation, Salvation is of Christ the Lord.

A PRAYER TO THE MOST HOLY TRINITY

O Most Holy Trinity, three Persons in one Almighty God,
we adore You, Who give life and vigor to every creature and
Who shed light eternal where there is darkness.
We offer You our hearts, our souls, and our whole being, today and
on the days to come, that we may offer perfect praise
and love to Your glorious Name.

O Father Almighty, we thank You for all the blessings
and graces You pour out upon us.

O merciful Christ Jesus, wash away our sins with Your
most precious blood. Make our hearts like Your own, we pray.
O dear Jesus, wipe away our tears and be with us,
O Lord, until our dying day.

O Holy Spirit, our guide and inspiration, lead us to the
right path. And on our way, when we encounter difficulties
and trials, we pray that You do not allow us to fall or lose hope.
Grant us the graces we need daily to live in
accordance with the holy will of God.
And when the time comes, O Holy Spirit, lead us into Paradise,
the place that is secure, full of joy and eternal peace. Amen.

ACT OF FAITH

O my God, I firmly believe that Thou art one God in Three Divine
Persons, Father, Son, and Holy Spirit. I believe that Thy Divine Son
became Man, and died for our sins, and that He will come to judge

the living and the dead. I believe these and all the truths which the Holy Catholic Church teaches, because Thou hast revealed them, Who can neither deceive nor be deceived. Amen.

ACT OF HOPE

O my God, relying on Thy almighty power and infinite mercy and promises, I hope to obtain pardon for my sins, the help of Thy grace, and life everlasting through the merits of Jesus Christ, my Lord and Redeemer. Amen.

ACT OF LOVE

O my God, I love Thee above all things, with my whole heart and soul, because Thou art all good and worthy of all love. I love my neighbor as myself for the love of Thee. I forgive all who have injured me, and ask pardon of all whom I have injured. Amen.

SAINT ANTHONY OF PADUA'S PRAYER TO THE LORD JESUS

Lord Jesus, make of us good and fertile soil, for the reception of the seed of Your grace, and make it yield worthy fruits of penance, so that with Your help we may merit to live eternally in Your glory, Who are blessed throughout all ages. Amen.

SAINT ANTHONY OF PADUA'S PRAYER TO THE HOLY SPIRIT

Holy Spirit, fire of love, come rest over each of us, make our tongues ready to confess our sins, that in revealing everything and concealing nothing, we may attain heavenly life to sing eternal praise with the angels, with Your help, You who live and reign through all ages. Amen.

SAINT FRANCIS' PRAYER IN PRAISE OF GOD

You are holy, Lord, the only God, and Your deeds are wonderful. You are strong. You are great. You are the Most High. You are Almighty. You, Holy Father, are King of heaven and earth. You are Three and One, Lord God, all Good. You are Good, all Good, supreme Good, Lord God, living and true.

You are Love. You are Wisdom. You are Humility.
You are Endurance. You are Rest. You are Peace.
You are Joy and Gladness. You are Justice and Moderation.
You are All our riches, and You suffice for us.
You are Beauty. You are Gentleness.

You are our Protector. You are our Guardian and Defender.
You are our Courage. You are our Haven and our Hope.
You are our Faith, our Great Consolation.
You are our Eternal Life, Great and Wonderful Lord,
God Almighty, Merciful Saviour. Amen.

A PRAYER OF SAINT FRANCIS OF ASSISI TO MARY

Holy Virgin Mary, there is none like you among
women born in the world.
Daughter and handmaid of the heavenly Father,
the Almighty King.
Mother of our Most High Lord Jesus Christ!
Spouse of the Holy Spirit!
Pray for us to your most Holy Son, our Lord and Master.

A PRAYER OF SAINT CATHERINE OF SIENA

Holy Spirit, come into my heart, draw it to Thee by Thy Power,
O my God, and grant me charity with filial fear. Preserve me,
O ineffable Love, from every evil thought; warm me with
Thy dear love, and every pain will seem light to me.
My Father, my sweet Lord, help me in all my actions.
Jesus, love, Jesus, love. Amen.

A PRAYER OF SAINT DOMINIC

May God the Father who made us bless us. May God the
Son send his healing among us. May God the Holy Spirit
move within us and give us eyes to see with, ears to hear
with, and hands that Your work might be done.
May we walk and preach the word of God to all.
May the angel of peace watch over us and lead
us at last by God's grace to the Kingdom. Amen.

COME HOLY SPIRIT

Come Holy Spirit, fill the hearts of Your faithful
and kindle in them the fire of Your love.
Send forth Your Spirit and they shall be created
and You shall renew the face of the earth.
O God, who by the light of the Holy Spirit
did instruct the hearts of the faithful, grant that by
the same Holy Spirit, we may be truly wise and ever
enjoy His consolation, through Christ the Lord. Amen.

THE APOSTLES CREED

I believe in God, the Father Almighty,
creator of heaven and earth.

I believe in Jesus Christ, His only Son, our Lord.
He was conceived by the power of the Holy Spirit
and was born of the Virgin Mary.
He suffered under Pontias Pilate,
was crucified, died, and was buried.
He descended into hell.
The third day He rose again from the dead.
He ascended into heaven,
and is seated at the right hand of the Father.
He will come again to judge the living and the dead.

I believe in the Holy Spirit,
the holy Catholic Church, the communion of saints,
the forgiveness of sins, the resurrection of the body,
and the life everlasting. Amen.

PRAYER OF AWE
BY SAINT CATHERINE OF SIENA

You, O eternal Trinity, are a deep sea into which,
the more I enter, the more I find.
And the more I find, the more I seek.

O abyss, O eternal Godhead, O sea profound,
what more could You give me than Yourself? Amen.

THE BIRTH OF JESUS CHRIST

"And it came to pass in those days, that there
went out a decree from Caesar Augustus,
that all the world should be taxed...And all went
to be taxed, every one into his own city.
And Joseph also went up from Galilee,
out of the city of Nazareth, into Judaea,
unto the city of David, which is called Bethlehem;
because he was of the house and lineage of David:
to be taxed with Mary his espoused wife, being great with child.
And so it was, that, while they were there, the days were
accomplished that she should be delivered.
And she brought forth her firstborn son, and wrapped him in
swaddling clothes, and laid him in a manger;
because there was no room for them in the inn."
Luke 2:1-7(KJV)

The Salvation of the world for which the Jewish people had been waiting for thousands of years was born in a small cave in Bethlehem. No kings or emperors were invited. Only Mary and Joseph witnessed the world shattering event.

There were heavenly fireworks and fanfare, but the world did not notice. The special star that rose in the sky at the moment of birth was unheeded by all except some foreigners from the East. The song of the "multitude of the heavenly host praising God" was heard only by some shepherds in the fields.

And after visiting the Holy Family that night, the shepherds told everyone they saw about what had happened to them. Those who heard "wondered at those things which were told them," but then their lives settled into their daily routines and, for most, the Ultimate was crowded out by the urgent. May we to whom the good news has been given, rejoice!

"For unto us a child is born, unto us a son is given" Isaiah 9:6.

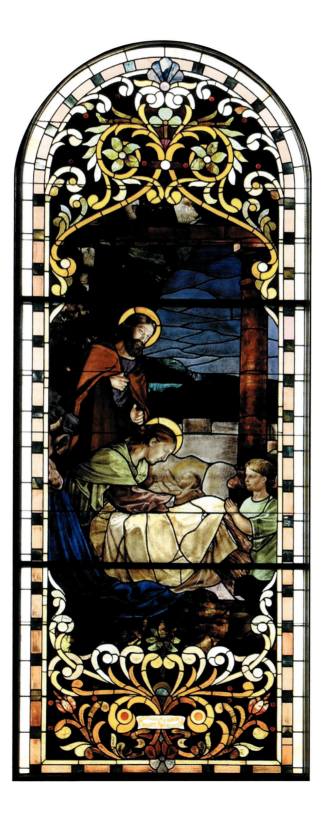

THE BIRTH OF JESUS CHRIST ICONOGRAPHY
Luke 2:1-20

Luke's account of the Birth of Christ records that Joseph and Mary, obeying a decree issued by Caesar Augustus, traveled from Nazareth to Bethlehem in order to be registered in the general census of the Roman Empire. While they were there, the time came for Mary to deliver: "And she gave birth to her first-born son and wrapped him in swaddling cloths, and laid him in a manger, because there was no place for them in the inn" (Luke 2:7).

The window scene includes the key figures of Joseph, Mary, and the Infant Jesus, as well as an adolescent boy. The Child is centrally placed in the composition while Mary, kneeling over the manger, lovingly embraces her firstborn. Joseph stands behind Mary and looks downward at his wife and child in his role as husband and protector of the family. A small child kneels near the manger with hands clasped in a gesture of adoration. On the far left edge of the window emerge the partially hidden heads of two humble animals, the ox and ass.

The Nativity holds the central position of Christian narratives in the visual arts, the earliest extant examples dating to the fourth century. Joseph is absent from these first depictions and even Mary may not be present. However, the ox and the ass, neither of which are mentioned in the biblical text, are always present and have continued to be a part of the popular and iconographic images of Nativity scenes ever since.

Theologians from the third century onward, beginning with Origen (185-232), related Isaiah's prophecy to the Bethlehem manger: "The ox knows its owner, and the ass its master's crib; but Israel does not know, my people do not understand" (Isaiah 1:3). These early church fathers, followed by Ambrose (c. 340-397) and Augustine (354-386), interpreted the ox as being the pure beast, the symbol of the chosen Jewish people, and the ass as the impure heathen peoples. Later interpretations associated the ass, because of its stubbornness, with the Jews and the ox with the Gentiles.

Although not identical, the figures and the general compositional setting of this window scene are closely modeled after a painting of the Nativity by the German artist Carl Müller (1839-1904). Müller's version includes an ensemble of shepherds and townspeople who have gathered to adore the Child. The Riordan artist who designed the window here achieved a more intimate and personal setting that encourages the viewer to join in the adoration of the Infant Jesus and the wonder of the Incarnation, by incorporating only key compositional elements from the original painting. In this window version, all but one onlooker have been eliminated. A single small child kneels to gaze closely on the wondrous birth.

The foreground area is illuminated by a brilliantly warm light that mystically emanates from the Christ Child and is the main light source for the image. The pictorial idea of the luminous Christ Child was inspired by a medieval text, *The Revelations of St. Bridget.* In this popular inspirational work of 1370, St. Bridget of Sweden (1303-1373) described Mary giving birth to her Son "...from whom radiated such an ineffable light and splendor, that the sun was not comparable to it ... ". St. Bridget's vision was extremely popular and had an immense influence on the depiction of Nativity scenes by Northern Renaissance and later Baroque artists.

Another iconographic element of the window, also taken from St. Bridget's vision, is the artist's treatment of Mary. St. Bridget described her as taking off her blue mantle, removing her shoes, and kneeling on the ground, dressed in a white tunic and adoring the Child.

"HOLY MARY, MOTHER OF GOD"
FROM DEUS CARITAS EST, POPE BENEDICT XVI

Mary, Virgin and Mother, shows us what love is
and whence it draws its origin and
its constantly renewed power.
To her we entrust the Church and
her mission in the service of love:

Holy Mary, Mother of God, you have given the world
its true light, Jesus, your Son - the Son of God.
You abandoned yourself completely to God's call
and this became a wellspring of the goodness
which flows forth from Him.

Show us Jesus. Lead us to Him. Teach us to know
and love Him, so that we too can become
capable of true love and be fountains
of living water in the midst of a thirsting world.

A PRAYER BY SAINT ELIZABETH ANN SETON

Lord Jesus, Who was born for us in a stable,
lived for us a life of pain and sorrow,
and died for us upon a cross; say to us,
"This day you shall be with Me in paradise."
Dear Saviour, leave us not, forsake us not.
We thirst for You, Fountain of Living Water.
Our days pass quickly along, soon all will be
consummated for us.
To Your hands we commend our spirits,
now and forever. Amen.

SALVE REGINA (HAIL, HOLY QUEEN)

Hail, Holy Queen, Mother of mercy!
Hail, our life, our sweetness and our hope!
To thee do we cry, poor banished children of Eve.
To thee do we send up our sighs, mourning and
weeping in this valley of tears.

Turn then, most gracious advocate, thine eyes of mercy
upon us and after this, our exile, show unto us
the blessed fruit of thy womb, Jesus.
O clement, O loving, O sweet Virgin Mary!

Pray for us O Holy Mother of God, that we may be
made worthy of the promises of Christ. Amen.

A CHRISTMAS PRAYER OF POPE JOHN XXIII

O sweet Child of Bethlehem, grant that we may share with
all our hearts in this profound mystery of Christmas.
Put into the hearts of men and women this peace
for which they sometimes seek so desperately and
which You alone can give to them.

Help them to know one another better, and to live
as brothers and sisters, children of the same Father.
Reveal to them also Your beauty, holiness and purity.

Awaken in their hearts love and gratitude
for Your infinite goodness.
Join them all together in Your love.
And give us Your heavenly peace. Amen.

"HAIL TO THEE! TRUE BODY SPRUNG" BY SAINT THOMAS AQUINAS

Hail to Thee! True body sprung from the Virgin Mary's womb!
The same that on the cross was hung and bore
for man the bitter doom.
Thou whose side was pierced and flowed
both with water and with blood;
Suffer us to taste of Thee in our life's last agony.
O kind, O loving One! O Jesus, Mary's Son! Amen.

PRAYER IN PRAISE OF CHRIST BY SAINT MELITO OF SARDIS, BISHOP AND MARTYR

Born as a son, led forth as a lamb, sacrificed as a sheep,
buried as a man, He rose from the dead as a God,
for He was by nature God and man.

He is all things: He judges and so He is Law;
He teaches, and so He is Wisdom;
He saves, and so He is Grace;
He begets, and so He is Father;
He is begotten, and so He is Son;
He suffers, and so He is Sacrifice;
He is buried, and so He is man;
He rises again, and so He is God.

This is Jesus Christ, to whom belongs glory for all ages. Amen.

A PRAYER OF SAINT CYRIL OF ALEXANDRIA

Hail, Mother and Virgin, imperishable Temple of the Godhead,
venerable treasure of the whole world,
crown of virginity, support of the true faith upon
which the Church is founded throughout the whole world.

Mother of God who inclosed under your heart the
infinite God, whom no space can contain.

Through you the Most Holy Trinity is adored and glorified,
demons are banished, Satan cast down from heaven into hell,
and our fallen nature again assumed into heaven.

Through you the human race, held captive in the bonds
of idolatry, arrives at the knowledge of the truth.

What more shall I say of you?
Hail, through whom kings rule, through whom
the only-begotten Son of God has become a star of light
to those who were sitting in darkness
and in the shadow of death! Amen.

A PRAYER OF SAINT JOHN VIANNEY

I love You, O my God, and my only desire is
to love You until the last breath of my life.
I love You, O my infinitely lovable God, and I would

rather die loving You, than live without loving You.
I love You, Lord, and the only grace
I ask is to love You eternally.
My God, if my tongue cannot say in every moment
that I love You, I want my heart to repeat it to
You as often as I draw breath. Amen.

A CHRISTMAS PRAYER

God of love, Father of all, the darkness that covered
the earth has given way to the bright dawn
of Your Word made flesh.
Make us a people of this light.
Make us faithful to Your Word, that we may bring
Your life to the waiting world.
Grant this through Christ our Lord. Amen.

GLORY TO GOD

Glory to God in the highest, and peace to His people on earth.
Lord God, heavenly King, Almighty God and Father,
we worship You, we give You thanks,
we praise You for Your glory.
Lord Jesus Christ, only Son of the Father, Lord God,
Lamb of God, You take away the sin
of the world: have mercy on us;
You are seated at the right hand of the Father: receive our prayer.
For You alone are the Holy One, You alone are the Lord,
You alone are the Most High, Jesus Christ,
with the Holy Spirit, in the glory of God the Father. Amen.

CHRIST, REDEEMER OF ALL
A 6TH CENTURY HYMN

Jesu, the Father's only Son,
whose death for all redemption won,
before the worlds, of God most high,
begotten all ineffably.
The Father's Light and Splendor Thou
their endless Hope to Thee that bow:

accept the prayers and praise today
that through the world Thy servants pay.

Salvation's author, call to mind
how, taking the form of humankind,
born of a Virgin undefiled,
Thou in man's flesh becamest a Child.

Thus testifies the present day
through every year in long array,
that Thou, salvation's source alone
proceedest from the Father's Throne.

Whence sky, and stars, and sea's abyss,
and earth, and all that therein is,
shall still, with laud and carol meet,
the Author of Thine Advent greet.

And we who, by Thy precious Blood
from sin redeemed, are marked for God,
on this, the day that saw Thy Birth,
sing the new song of ransomed earth.

All honor, laud, and glory be,
O Jesu, Virgin-born, to Thee;
whom with the Father we adore,
and Holy Ghost forevermore. Amen.

ALMA REDEMPTORIS MATER
(LOVING MOTHER OF THE REDEEMER)

Loving mother of the Redeemer, gate of heaven,
star of the sea, assist your people who have fallen
yet strive to rise again.

To the wonderment of nature you bore
your Creator, yet remained a virgin after as before.
You who received Gabriel's joyful greeting,
have pity on us poor sinners. Amen.

THE RESURRECTION
MATTHEW 28:1-10; MARK 16:1-18;
LUKE 24:1-49; JOHN 20:1-29
IF JESUS DID NOT RISE FROM THE DEAD, OUR FAITH IS IN VAIN

In Gethsemane the disciples gathered up their cloaks and ran scared, straight away from Jesus. Peter, who had sworn just a few hours earlier that he would follow his Master to the death, skulked in the shadows and, when confronted, swore violently that he did not know the Man. John eventually found his way to the cross, but had no words as he watched his Master and friend gasp raggedly for breath, His tattered body bleeding and torn.

The two disciples walking along the road to Emmaus expressed the shattered dreams of Jesus' followers: "the chief priests and our rulers delivered him to the sentence of death and crucified him; but we were hoping that it was he who was going to redeem Israel" (Luke 24:20-21). The Eleven hid in a locked room, afraid of the authorities. Their disillusionment was so deep that when Mary Magdalen and others reported having seen the risen Christ, most did not believe them (Mark 16:11).

As the disciples soon learned, Jesus Christ has risen from the dead and is alive. Because of Christ's resurrection, Christians know there is a world beyond the grave. The empty tomb confirms that God the Father has accepted Christ's sacrifice for our sins and has reconciled us to Himself.

""Why do you seek the living among the dead? Remember how he told you, while he was still in Galilee that the Son of man must be delivered into the hands of sinful men, and be crucified and on the third day rise.' And they remembered his words." Luke 24:5-8

A confident Peter was able to say, fifty days later in Jerusalem: "Let all the house of Israel therefore know assuredly that God has made him both Lord and Christ, this Jesus whom you crucified" (Acts 2:36).

THE RESURRECTION ICONOGRAPHY
Matthew 28:1-20; Mark 16:1-8;
Luke 24:1-12; and John 20:1-20

That Jesus rose from the dead on the third day after His Crucifixion is a fundamental tenet of Christian belief and the crowning truth of the Christian faith. Professed in the Apostles' Creed, "on the third day he rose from the dead," all four Gospels present the Resurrection as a factual physical event. There were no eyewitnesses, nor are there any scriptural descriptions, of the actual event. Nevertheless, depictions of this transcendent event are abundant in the history of art. A number of different aspects and variations of the event have been created.

The Gospel of Matthew states that the chief priests and the Pharisees were fearful that Christ's disciples would steal the body away and tell the people "He has risen from the dead ..." (Matthew 27:64). Therefore, they asked Pilate to secure the tomb. Pilate replied: " You have a guard of soldiers; go, make it as secure as you can" (Matthew 27:65). So they went and secured the tomb by "sealing the stone and setting a guard" (Matthew 7:66).

The Resurrection window illustrates Matthew's account of the Resurrection. In the lower zone of the window two Roman soldiers crouch in front of the empty tomb, blinded by a blazing light. Their postures faithfully recall the gospel account of their fear, so great that they trembled and became like dead men, when an angel of the Lord announced "He is not here; for he has risen ... Come, see the place where he lay" (Mathew 28:6).

Above the two guards, a triumphant Christ steps out of His tomb, encased in a radiant divine light and surrounded by clouds, an attribute of heaven. Wrapped in a gleaming white gown, His right hand is raised upward and victoriously points toward Heaven. His left hand carries the Resurrection staff bearing a red banner emblazoned with a white Latin cross, symbolic of His victory over death. The Resurrection scene constitutes the confirmation of all Christ's works and teachings and is the ultimate and defining proof of His divinity.

EASTER PRAYER OF SAINT HIPPOLYTUS

Christ is risen: the world below lies desolate;
Christ is risen: the spirits of evil are fallen;
Christ is risen: the angels of God are rejoicing;
Christ is risen: the tombs of the dead are empty;
Christ is risen indeed from the dead,
the first of sleepers,

Glory and power are His forever and ever. Amen.

RESURRECTION PRAYER

O Risen Lord, the Way, the Truth and the Life, make
us faithful followers of the spirit of Your resurrection.

Grant that we may be inwardly renewed; dying
to ourselves in order that You may live in us.

May our lives serve as signs of the
transforming power of Your love.

Use us as Your instruments for the renewal
of society, bringing Your life and love to all
and leading them to Your Church.

This we ask of You, Lord Jesus, living and
reigning with the Father, in the unity of
the Holy Spirit, God forever. Amen.

REGINA CAELI

Rejoice, O Queen of Heaven, Alleluia!
For He whom thou didst merit to bear, Alleluia!
Has risen as He said, Alleluia!
Pray for us to God, Alleluia!

V. Rejoice and be glad, O Virgin Mary, Alleluia!
R. For the Lord has risen indeed, Alleluia!

Let us pray: O God, Who hast given joy to

the whole world through the Resurrection
of Thy Son, our Lord Jesus Christ; grant that
through the prayers of His Virgin Mother Mary,
we may obtain the joys of everlasting life.
Through the same Christ, our Lord. Amen.

ADORAMUS TE OF SAINT FRANCIS OF ASSISI

We adore Thee, most holy Lord Jesus Christ, here
and in all Thy churches that are in the whole world,
and we bless Thee; because by Thy Holy Cross
Thou hast redeemed the world. Amen.

JESUS, BREAD OF HEAVEN

Jesus, Bread of Heaven come,
Come, Lord Jesus, Come.
Make my soul more like Your own,
Come, Lord Jesus, Come.
Help me always to do right,
Come, Lord Jesus, Come.
Keep me from the stain of sin,
Come, Lord Jesus, Come.

FATIMA PRAYER

O my Jesus, forgive us our sins, save us from
the fires of Hell, lead all souls to Heaven, and help
especially those most in need of Thy mercy. Amen.

JESUS PRAYER

Lord Jesus Christ, Son of God,
have mercy on me, a sinner. Amen.

A PRAYER TO JESUS BY SAINT PIO OF PIETRELCINA

Lord, God of my heart, You alone know and see all
my troubles. You alone are aware that all my distress
springs from my fear of losing You, of offending You,

from my fear of not loving You as much as I
should love and desire to love You.

If You, to whom everything is present and
who alone can see the future, know that it is for
Your greater glory and for my salvation
that I should remain in this state, then let it be so.
I do not want to escape from it.
Give me the strength to fight and to obtain
the prize due to strong souls. Amen.

A PRAYER OF SAINT AUGUSTINE OF HIPPO

Lord Jesus, let me know myself and know You,
and desire nothing save only You.
Let me hate myself and love You.
Let me do everything for the sake of You.
Let me humble myself and exalt You.
Let me think of nothing except You.
Let me die to myself and live in You.
Let me accept whatever happens as from You.
Let me banish self and follow You,
and ever desire to follow You.
Let me fly from myself and take refuge in You,
that I may deserve to be defended by You.
Let me fear for myself, let me fear You, and let me
be among those who are chosen by You.
Let me distrust myself and put my trust in You.
Let me be willing to obey for the sake of You.
Let me cling to nothing save only to You,
and let me be poor because of You.
Look upon me, that I may love You.
Call me that I may see You,
and forever enjoy You. Amen.

ANIMA CHRISTI

Soul of Christ, sanctify me.
Body of Christ, save me.
Blood of Christ, inebriate me.
Water from the side of Christ, wash me.

Passion of Christ, strengthen me.
O good Jesus, hear me.
Within Your wounds hide me.
Suffer me not to be separated from You.
From the malicious enemy defend me.
At the hour of death, call me
and bid me come close to You
That with Your saints I may praise You,
forever and ever. Amen.

A PRAYER OF SAINT AMBROSE

O Lord, Who has mercy upon all, take away from me my sins,
and mercifully kindle in me the fire of Your Holy Spirit.
Take away from me the heart of stone:
give me a heart of flesh, a heart to love, to adore You,
Lord, a heart to delight in You, to follow, to rejoice in You,
for the sake of Jesus Christ. Amen.

SAINT GREGORY THE GREAT'S EASTER PRAYER

It is only right, with all the powers of our heart and mind,
to praise You, Father, and Your Only-Begotten Son,
Our Lord Jesus Christ.
Dear Father, by Your wondrous condescension
of loving-kindness toward us, Your servants,
You gave up Your Son.
Dear Jesus, You paid the debt of Adam
for us to the Eternal Father by
Your Blood poured forth in loving-kindness.
You cleared away the darkness of sin
by Your magnificent and radiant Resurrection.
You broke the bonds of death and rose
from the grave as a Conqueror.
You reconciled heaven and earth.
Our life had no hope of eternal happiness
before You redeemed us.
Your Resurrection has washed away our sins,
restored our innocence and brought us to joy.

How inestimable is the tenderness of Your Love. Amen.

THE IMMACULATE CONCEPTION, PREDESTINED FROM ETERNITY AND UNIQUELY PREPARED TO BE THE DWELLING PLACE OF GOD

In 1854, Pope Pius IX formally defined the Immaculate Conception: "The most Blessed Virgin Mary was, from the first moment of her conception, by a singular grace and privilege of almighty God and by virtue of the merits of Jesus Christ, Saviour of the human race, preserved from all stain of original sin" (*Ineffabilis Deus*).

The angel Gabriel greeted Mary, "Hail, full of grace, the Lord is with you." Luke 1:28. The phrase, "full of grace," a translation of the Greek word, *kecharitomene*, indicates that Mary was in a state of sanctifying grace from the first moment of her existence.

In continuity with scriptural witness and Christian tradition, it is affirmed that Mary is saved by the redemptive work of Jesus Christ alone and is "blessed among women" to be the New Eve who bears the New Adam, the Saviour of the world. She is sinless only by virtue of the saving work of Christ.

Lourdes has become the most famous shrine of Our Lady. It was there that the Virgin Mary in 1858 appeared eighteen times in the grotto of Massabielle to a young peasant girl, Bernadette Soubirous. When Bernadette asked her vision for a name, Mary replied, "I am the Immaculate Conception." She asked that a chapel be built on the site of the vision and told the girl to drink from a fountain in the grotto. No fountain was to be seen, but when Bernadette began to dig, a miraculous freshwater spring began flowing at the grotto.

On December 8, 1933, the feast of the Immaculate Conception, Bernadette was declared a Saint by Pope Pius XI. The incorrupt body of Saint Bernadette remains in the main chapel of the Convent of Saint Gildard in Nevers, France. Around her shrine are inscribed the words of the great promise made to her by the Blessed Virgin Mary at Lourdes:

"I do not promise that you will be happy in this world, only in the next."

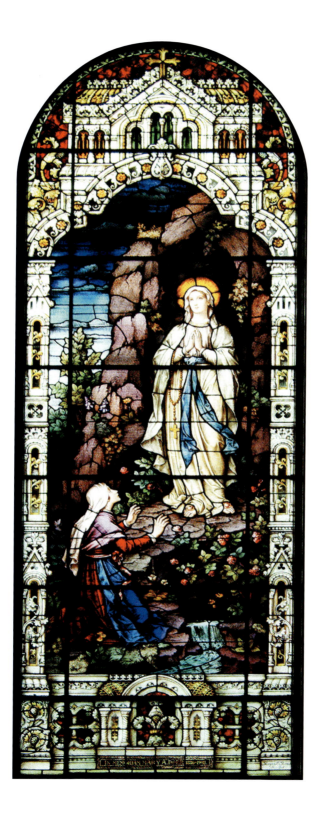

IN MEMORIAM MARY A. DOER 1835-1901

OUR LADY OF LOURDES ICONOGRAPHY

On February 11, 1858, a fourteen-year old girl named Bernadette Soubirous (1844-79) was gathering wood near her home in the Pyrenees Mountains in southern France. In the grotto of a rocky cliff near Lourdes, the Grotto of Massabielle, she saw a vision of a young Lady.

Bernadette described the appearance of the Lady as young and beautiful, dressed in white with a blue sash. A golden rosary hung over her arm and golden roses graced her bare feet. The Lady asked for prayers, penance, the conversion of sinners, and also for a chapel to be built at the grotto. On March 25, the Lady identified herself as the "Immaculate Conception."

The Mayer artist of the Lourdes window has accurately followed the testimony of young Bernadette in his depiction of the Blessed Virgin Mary. She is elegantly dressed in a simple white gown and mantle. At her waist is a blue sash blowing gently in the breeze. Blue, the color associated with Mary, is the color in which she appears throughout the window program. A yellow rosary hangs noticeably from her right arm and a brilliant nimbus, or halo, illuminates her head. Each of her feet is topped by a single pink and golden rose.

Looking upward with hands clasped at her breast, the Virgin is enveloped by the natural rock of the grotto, from which grows an attractive variety of spring flowers, all of which possess Marian symbolism. The yellow daisy, located just to her right, is visible growing from the upper ledge of the grotto as well as the lower left foreground. This flower symbolizes her purity and innocence. Also found on the upper grotto ledge is a lavender foxglove, a flower associated with youthfulness as well as healing. Foxglove is known as "Our Lady's Gloves." The rose, like the lily, is one of the principal Marian symbols and figures prominently in this scene. Pink rose bushes, bearing a plentitude of blooms, surround her. On her feet are roses sharing the colors pink and yellow. On the rosary, the Glorious Mysteries are symbolized by the yellow or golden rose.

In the lower left area of the window, a cool spring of water gushes from underneath the grotto. On February 25, 1857, the Lady commanded Bernadette to got and drink from and then to wash in a stream inside the grotto. Bernadette was able to get a few handfuls of water from a patch that was little more than muddy ground. After the Apparition, the muddy water soon became a spring and quickly developed into a fountain of free-flowing water.

Bernadette is depicted in the window as a young peasant girl. In 1866, Bernadette joined the Sisters of Charity at Nevers, where she remained until her death in 1879. She was canonized in 1933, by Pope Pius XI. Her incorrupt body remains on display in Nevers.

AN ASPIRATION TO MARY BY SAINT ALPHONSUS LIGUORI

O Mary, conceived without sin, pray for us who have recourse to thee. Holy Mary, pray for us!

Immaculate Heart of Mary, pray for us now and at the hour of our death.

Sweet Heart of Mary, be my salvation! Our Lady, Queen of Peace, pray for us. Amen.

THE DIVINE PRAISES

Blessed be God. Blessed be His Holy Name.
Blessed be Jesus Christ, true God and true Man.
Blessed be the Name of Jesus.
Blessed be His Most Sacred Heart.
Blessed be His Most Precious Blood.
Blessed be Jesus in the Most Holy Sacrament of the Altar.
Blessed be the Holy Ghost, the Paraclete.
Blessed be the great Mother of Christ, Mary most Holy.
Blessed be her Holy and Immaculate Conception.
Blessed be her Glorious Assumption.
Blessed be the Name of Mary, Virgin and Mother.
Blessed be St. Joseph, her most chaste spouse.
Blessed be God in His Angels and in His Saints.

A SOLEMN ACT OF CONSECRATION TO THE IMMACULATE HEART OF MARY BY VENERABLE POPE PIUS XII

Most Holy Virgin Mary, tender Mother of men,
to fulfill the desires of the Sacred Heart of Jesus
and the request of the vicar of your Son on earth,
we consecrate ourselves and our families
to your Sorrowful and Immaculate Heart,
O Queen of the Most Holy Rosary,
and we recommend to you, all the people
of our country and all the world.

Please accept our consecration, dearest Mother, and use us as you wish to accomplish your designs in the world.

O Sorrowful and Immaculate Heart of Mary,
Queen of the Most Holy Rosary, and Queen of the World,
rule over us, together with the Sacred Heart of Jesus Christ,
Our King, save us from the spreading flood
of modern paganism; kindle in our hearts and homes
the love of purity, the practice of a virtuous life,
an ardent zeal for souls, and a desire
to pray the Rosary more faithfully.

We come with confidence to you, O Throne of Grace and
Mother of Fair Love. Inflame us with the same Divine Fire
which has inflamed your own Sorrowful and Immaculate Heart.
Make our hearts and homes your shrine, and through us,
make the Heart of Jesus, together with your rule,
triumph in every heart and home. Amen.

POPE BLESSED JOHN PAUL II'S PRAYER TO OUR LADY OF LOURDES

Hail Mary, poor and humble woman, blessed by the Most High!
Virgin of hope, dawn of a new era, we join in your song of praise,
to celebrate the Lord's mercy, to proclaim the coming of
the Kingdom and the full liberation of humanity.

Hail Mary, lowly handmaid of the Lord, Glorious Mother of Christ!
Faithful Virgin, holy dwelling-place of the Word, teach
us to persevere in listening to the Word, and to be
docile to the voice of the Spirit, attentive to His
promptings in the depths of our conscience and to His
manifestations in the events of history.

Hail Mary, Woman of Sorrows, Mother of the living! Virgin spouse
beneath the Cross, the new Eve, be our guide along the
paths of the world. Teach us to experience and to spread
the love of Christ, to stand with you before the
innumerable crosses on which your Son is still crucified.

Hail Mary, woman of faith, first of the disciples!
Virgin Mother of the Church, help us always to account for
the hope that is in us, with trust in human goodness
and the Father's love. Teach us to build up the
world beginning from within: in the depths of

silence and prayer, in the joy of fraternal love,
in the unique fruitfulness of the Cross.

Holy Mary, Mother of believers,
Our Lady of Lourdes, pray for us. Amen.

EXCERPT FROM THE WRITINGS OF SAINT MAXIMILIAN MARY KOBE

The Immaculate One appears in this world without the
least stain of sin, the masterpiece of God's hands, full of grace.
God, the Most Holy Trinity, beholds the lowliness
(that is, the humility, the root of all her other virtues)
of His handmaid, and does great things for her, He the Almighty.
God the Father gives her His own Son to be her Son;
God the Son descends into her womb; and God the Holy Spirit
forms the body of Christ in the womb of this pure Virgin.
And the Word was made flesh (Jn.1,14).

The Immaculate One becomes the Mother of God.
The fruit of the love of God in His Trinitarian life and
of Mary the Immaculate One is Christ the God-Man.

MARY IMMACULATE, STAR OF THE MORNING

Mary Immaculate, star of the morning,
chosen before the creation began,
chosen to bring, for thy bridal adorning,
woe to the serpent and rescue to man.

Here, in an orbit of shadow and sadness,
veiling thy splendor, thy course thou hast run;
now thou art throned in all glory and gladness,
crowned by the hand of thy Saviour and Son.

Sinners, we worship thy sinless perfection;
fallen and weak, for thy pity we plead;
grant us the shield of thy sovereign protection,
measure thine aid by the depth of our need.

Frail is our nature, and strict our probation,
watchful the foe that would lure us to wrong;

succor our souls in the hour of temptation,
Mary Immaculate, tender and strong.

See how the wiles of the serpent assail us,
see how we waver and flinch in the fight;
let thine immaculate merit avail us,
make of our weakness a proof of thy might.

Bend from thy throne at the voice of our crying,
bend to this earth which thy footsteps have trod;
stretch out thine arms to us, living and dying,
Mary Immaculate, Mother of God.

PRAYER AT THE LOURDES GROTTO IN THE VATICAN GARDENS

O blessed Virgin, Mother of God, Mother of Christ, Mother
of the Church, look upon us mercifully at this hour.
Virgin faithful, pray for us.

Teach us to believe as you believed. Make our faith
in God, in Christ, in the Church, always to be
serene, courageous, strong, and generous.
Mother worthy of love, Mother of faithful love, pray for us.

Teach us to love God and our brothers and sisters as
you loved them: make our love for others to be always
patient, kindly, and respectful. Cause of our joy, pray for us.

Teach us to be able to grasp, in faith, the paradox of
Christian joy, which springs up and blooms from sorrow,
renunciation, and union with your sacrificed Son.
Make our joy to be always genuine and full,
in order to be able to communicate it to all. Amen.

A PRAYER TO OUR LADY OF LOURDES

Holy Virgin Mary Immaculate, Mother of God and our Mother,
speak thou for us to the Heart of Jesus,
Who is thy Son and our Brother.
Our Lady of Lourdes, pray for us. Amen.

A MARIAN PRAYER OF SAINT GERMANUS, BISHOP OF AUXERRE

Hail Mary, full of grace, more holy than the saints,
more elevated than the heavens,
more glorious than the angels,
and more venerable than every creature.

Hail heavenly paradise, all fragrant and
a lily that gives off the sweetest scent,
a perfumed rose that opens up for
the health of mortals.

Hail immaculate temple of the Lord,
constructed in a holy fashion,
ornament of Divine magnificence,
open to everyone, and oasis of mystical delicacies.

Hail mountain of shade, grazing ground for the holy Lamb
who takes upon Himself the miseries and sins of all.

Hail sacred throne of God, blessed dwelling,
sublime ornaments, precious jewel, and
splendiferous heavens.

Hail urn of purest gold, who contained the
manna Christ, the gentle sweetness of our souls.

Hail most pure Virgin Mother, worthy of praise
and veneration, fount of gushing waters,
treasure of innocence, and splendor of sanctity.

O Mary, lead us to the port of peace and salvation,
to the glory of Christ who lives in eternity
with the Father and with the Holy Spirit. Amen.

A FATIMA PRAYER

Oh my Jesus, I offer this for love of Thee, for the
conversion of sinners, and in reparation for the sins
committed against the Immaculate Heart of Mary. Amen.

THE ANNUNCIATION
LUKE 1: 26-38
"BEHOLD, I AM THE HANDMAID OF THE LORD."

Mary learned from the angel Gabriel that God wished her to be the mother of God and she humbly accepted. By her 'fiat,' Jesus, the Light of the World, is incarnate. Through the virgin Mary, salvation comes, not from human beings and their powers, but solely from God - from an act of His grace.

"the angel Gabriel was sent from God to a city of Galilee named Nazareth, to a virgin betrothed to a man whose name was Joseph, of the house of David; and the virgin's name was Mary.
And he came to her and said, '
Hail, full of grace, The Lord is with you!'
But she was greatly troubled at the saying and considered in her mind what sort of greeting this might be.
Then the angel said to her,
'Do not be afraid, Mary, for you have found favor with God.
And behold, you will conceive in your womb and bear a son, and you shall call his name Jesus.
He will be great, and will be called the Son of the Most High; and the Lord God will give to him the throne of his father David, and he will reign over the house of Jacob for ever; and of his kingdom there will be no end.'
And Mary said to the angel,
'How shall this be, since I have no husband?'
And the angel said to her, 'The Holy Spirit will come upon you, and the power of the Most High will overshadow you; therefore the child to be born will be called holy, the Son of God. And behold, your kinswoman Elizabeth in her old age has also conceived a son; and this is the sixth month with her who was called barren. For with God nothing will be impossible.'
And Mary said, 'Behold, I am the handmaid of the Lord; Let it be to me according to your word.'

Lord, not our will, but Your will be done.

IN MEMORIAM JOHN D. McCARTHY · ANNIE E McCARTHY

THE ANNUNCIATION ICONOGRAPHY
Luke 1:26-38

The Annunciation window reveals the moment when the Archangel Gabriel announces to Mary that she is to be the mother of Christ, as described in the Gospel of Luke: "Hail, full of grace, the Lord is with you ... The Holy Spirit will come upon you, and the power of the Most High will overshadow you; therefore the child to be born will be called holy, the Son of God" (Luke 1:28, 35).

This rendering is modeled after traditional Western interpretations of the Annunciation. Entering the room from the left, Gabriel is dressed in white which is a symbol of purity and bears magnificent blue wings. His right hand is raised in a gesture of blessing toward the Virgin, while his left hand grasps a red scepter which identifies him as the herald of God.

An attribute of Gabriel is the lily, or fleur-de-lis, topping his staff of authority. This flower is the principal symbol of purity and chastity and is closely associated with the Virgin Mary, especially in Annunciation scenes. The large vase of white lilies prominently placed in the lower left foreground points to Mary at the Annunciation, but also prefigures the Easter lily, illustrating the truth that within the Incarnation of Christ exists the Christ of the Resurrection.

The Annunciation window introduces the Virgin wearing a white tunic and blue mantle, which she wears throughout the remainder of the Franz Mayer narrative program. This visually identifies her personage. Indicative of her youthfulness, her long hair flows freely down her back while a golden nimbus, filled with white stars, symbolizes her state of grace. The star-filled nimbus, or halo, is drawn from the description in Revelation 12:1.

Mary kneels before an intricately carved prie-dieu, arms lightly folded across her breast, indicating her modesty and willing acceptance of Gabriel's message and the blessing from God. A book lies open before her as a reminder of her precocious understanding of the sacred Scriptures. She is depicted reading from a book, thus referring to Isaiah's prophecy: "Behold, a young woman shall conceive and bear a son, and shall call his name Immanuel" (Isaiah 7:14).

A reference to the fulfillment of this prophecy is symbolized by the carved owls located on the back of the prie-dieu. The owl, a bird of night and darkness, here functions as an attribute of Christ who sacrificed Himself to save mankind: "To give light to those who sit in darkness and in the shadow of death, to guide our feet" (Luke 1:79).

Behind Mary is a baldachin or canopy over a tabernacle, another reference to Mary, the Tabernacle of God. Just as the tabernacle on the altar houses the Blessed Sacrament, Mary by her "fiat" houses the Incarnate Christ. The presence of the altar and closed tabernacle also prefigures the future sacrifice of Christ. The Eucharistic theme is further emphasized by the clusters of grapes.

Lastly, the white dove hovering above this miraculous scene and encased within an aureole of divine light symbolizes the presence of the Holy Spirit (John 1:32). Diagonal rays emanating downward and resting directly above Mary's head symbolize the moment of the Incarnation when Christ, anointed by the Holy Spirit, is conceived as man in the womb of the Virgin Mary.

THE ANGELUS

V: The Angel of the Lord declared unto Mary
R: And she conceived by the Holy Spirit.

V: Hail Mary, full of grace: The Lord is with thee.
Blessed art thou among women and blessed
is the fruit of thy womb, Jesus.
R: Holy Mary, Mother of God: Pray for us sinners now
and at the hour of our death. Amen.

V: Behold, the handmaid of the Lord.
R: Be it done to me according to thy word.

V: Hail Mary, full of grace: The Lord is with thee.
Blessed are thou among women and blessed
is the fruit of thy womb, Jesus.
R: Holy Mary, Mother of God: Pray for us sinners now
and at the hour of our death. Amen.

V: And the Word was made flesh
R: And dwelt among us.

V: Hail Mary, full of grace: The Lord is with thee.
Blessed art thou among women and blessed
is the fruit of thy womb, Jesus.
R: Holy Mary, Mother of God: Pray for us sinners now
and at the hour of our death. Amen.

V: Pray for us, O holy Mother of God,
R: That we may be made worthy of the promises of Christ.

V: Let us pray.

ALL: Pour forth, we beseech thee, O Lord, Thy grace into our
hearts, that we, to whom the Incarnation of Christ, thy Son,
was made known by the message of an Angel,

may by His Passion and Cross be brought to the glory of His
Resurrection, through the same Christ, our Lord, Amen.

SUB TUUM PRAESIDIUM
[oldest known prayer to the Virgin, first found in a
Greek papyrus c.300 AD]

We turn to you for protection, Holy Mother of God.
Listen to our prayers and help us in our needs.
Save us from every danger, glorious and blessed Virgin.

A PRAYER TO MARY OF SAINT BERNARD OF CLAIRVAUX

By you we have access to your Son, O blessed finder of grace,
Mother of Life, Mother of Salvation,
that by you He may receive us, who by you was given to us. Amen.

A PRAYER OF SAINT ALBERT THE GREAT

"Fear not, Mary, for thou hast found grace with God." (Luke 1:30).

Fear not, Mary, for you have found, not taken
grace, as Lucifer tried to take it.
You have not lost it, as Adam lost it.
You have found it because you have
desired and sought it.
You have found uncreated grace:
that is, God Himself became your Son,
and with that grace you have found
and obtained every uncreated good. Amen.

SAINT FRANCIS OF ASSISI'S PRAYER PRAISING
MARY THE MOTHER OF GOD

Hail, O Lady, Holy Queen, Mary holy Mother of God:
you are the Virgin made Church chosen by
the most Holy Father in heaven whom he consecrated

with His most holy beloved Son and with
the Holy Spirit the Paraclete, in whom there was
and is all fullness of grace and every good thing.

Hail His Palace! Hail His Tabernacle!
Hail His Dwelling! Hail His Robe!
Hail His Servant! Hail His Mother!

And hail all you holy virtues which are poured into
the hearts of the faithful through the grace and
enlightenment of the Holy Spirit, that from being
unbelievers, you may make them faithful to God. Amen.

"PRAYER TO OUR LADY, MOTHER OF MERCY"
BY SAINT AUGUSTINE OF HIPPO

Blessed Virgin Mary, who can worthily repay you
with praise and thanksgiving for having rescued
a fallen world by your generous consent!
Receive our gratitude, and by your prayers
obtain the pardon of our sins.

Take our prayers into the sanctuary of heaven
and enable them to make our peace with God.

Holy Mary, help the miserable, strengthen the
discouraged, comfort the sorrowful,
pray for your people, pledge for the clergy,
intercede for all women consecrated to God.

May all who venerate you feel now your help and protection.
Be ready to help us when we pray,
and bring back to us the answers to our prayers.

Make it your continual concern to pray
for the people of God, for you were blessed by God

and were made worthy to bear the Redeemer
of the world, who lives and reigns forever. Amen.

PRAYER FOR INTERCESSION TO SAINT GABRIEL

O Blessed Archangel Gabriel, we beseech thee,
do thou intercede for us at the throne
of Divine Mercy in our present necessities.
That as thou didst announce to Mary the mystery of
the Incarnation, so through thy prayers and patronage
in heaven we may obtain the benefits of the same, and sing
the praise of God forever in the land of the living. Amen.

"MARY, VIRGIN MOST POWERFUL" BY POPE SAINT PIUS X

Let the storm rage and the sky darken -
not for that shall we be dismayed.
If we trust as we should in Mary, we shall recognize
in her, the Virgin Most Powerful "who with virginal foot
did crush the head of the serpent."

MEMORARE

Remember, most loving Virgin Mary, never was it heard that
anyone who turned to you for help was left unaided.
Inspired by this confidence though burdened by my sins,
I run to your protection for you are my mother.
Mother of the Word of God, do not despise my words of
pleading, but be merciful and hear my prayer. Amen.

AVE MARIS STELLA

Hail, Star of the sea!	Ave, maris stella!
Blessed Mother of God,	Dei mater alma,
yet ever a Virgin!	atque semper virgo!
O happy gate of heaven.	Felix caeli porta.

Thou that didst receive	Sumens illud Ave
the Ave from Gabriel's lips,	Gabrielis ore,
confirm us in peace,	funda nos in pace,
and so let Eva be changed	mutans Evae nomen.
into an Ave of blessing for us.	
Loose the sinner's chains,	Solve vincla reis,
bring light to the blind,	profer lumen caecis,
drive from us our evils,	mala nostra pelle,
and ask all good things for us.	bona cuncta posce.
Show thyself a Mother,	Monstra te esse
and offer our prayers to Him,	matrem, sumat per te
who would be born of thee,	preces, qui pro nobis
when born for us.	natus, tulit esse tuus.
O incomparable Virgin,	Virgo singularis,
and meekest of the meek,	inter omnes mitis,
obtain us the forgiveness of our sins,	nos culpis solutos
and make us meek and chaste.	mites fac et castos.
Obtain us purity of life,	Vitam praesta puram,
and a safe pilgrimage;	iter pare tutum;
that we may be united with thee,	ut videntes Jesum,
in the blissful vision of Jesus.	semper collaetemur.
Praise be to God the Father,	Sit laus Deo Patri,
and to the Lord Jesus	summo Christo decus,
and to the Holy Spirit:	Spiritui Sancto,
to the three one self-same praise.	tribus honor unus.
V. Hail Mary, full of grace, alleluia.	Ave Maria, gratia plena, alleluia.
R. The Lord be with you, alleluia.	Dominus tecum, alleluia.

THE VISITATION
LUKE 1:39-56
"MY SOUL PROCLAIMS THE GREATNESS OF THE LORD"

When the angel Gabriel visited Mary to seek her "yes" to God's Plan of Salvation, he told her that her cousin, Elizabeth, an elderly woman and barren, had conceived because "nothing will be impossible for God." Mary's first action was to travel to help her cousin during the last three months of her pregnancy with the baby who would become known as "John the Baptist."

Mary greeted Elizabeth, who "cried out in a loud voice,"

"'Blessed are you among women, and blessed
is the fruit of your womb! And why is this granted me,
that the mother of my Lord should come to me?
For behold, when the voice of your greeting came to
my ears, the babe in my womb leaped for joy.
And blessed is she who believed that there would be a
fulfillment of what was spoken to her from the Lord.'"

"And Mary said: 'My soul magnifies the Lord, and my
spirit rejoices in God my Saviour, for he has regarded
the low estate of his handmaiden. For behold,
henceforth all generations will call me blessed; for he
who is mighty has done great things for me,
and holy is his name. And his mercy is on those who
fear him from generation to generation.
He has shown strength with his arm, he has scattered the
proud in the imagination of their hearts, he has put
down the mighty from their thrones, and
exalted those of low degree;
he has filled the hungry with good things,
and the rich he has sent empty away.
He has helped his servant Israel, in remembrance
of his mercy, as he spoke to our fathers,
to Abraham and to his posterity for ever.'"

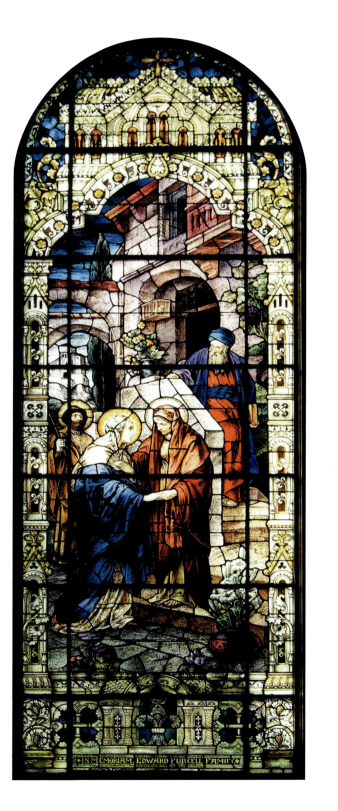

IN MEMORIAM EDWARD PURCELL FAMILY

THE VISITATION ICONOGRAPHY
Luke 1:39-56

After the Annunciation, Mary traveled to the hill country of Judea to visit her cousin Elizabeth. Although well past child-bearing age, Elizabeth was also expecting her firstborn. The archangel Gabriel had prophesied to Zachariah, Elizabeth's husband, that their child would be filled with the Holy Spirit and would prepare the people for the coming of the Lord (Luke 1: 13-17).

The window scene unfolds in front of the stone home of Elizabeth and Zachariah. It features the two favored women warmly embracing each other. Elizabeth does not have any specific iconography, but is always depicted as an older woman. Dressed in matronly attire, she stands at the bottom of the porch steps with both arms extended in a gesture of welcome to the younger Mary.

The Gospel of Luke describes how, when Elizabeth heard Mary's greeting, the Holy Spirit produced a remarkable response in her unborn baby and in her: "the babe leaped in her womb; and Elizabeth was filled with the Holy Spirit" (Luke 1:41). Elizabeth greets Mary with a gladness and humility suitable for one who recognizes the Mother of her Lord: "Blessed are you among women, and blessed is the fruit of your womb!" (Luke 1:42).

Mary is clothed primarily in blue, the color most associated with the Blessed Virgin. Her robe underneath the cloak has a fleur-de-lis pattern woven into the white and gold fabric. These colors are both associated with purity and divinity, pointing perhaps to the Divine within her womb. The fleur-de-lis, associated with Mary, is also a symbol of the Trinity.

In addition to the two women, Joseph and Zachariah are included in this depiction although neither is mentioned in Luke's narrative. Joseph is located directly behind Mary and is dressed in yellow, a color with which he is typically associated. His hat and staff reveal that he has traveled a distance.

Depicted as an old man with a long white beard, Zachariah walks out the front door and begins to descend the steps. He carries a book and wears a blue turban and sash, all of which refer to his priestly profession.

The caged white turtledove, hanging in the doorway close to Zachariah, serves to reinforce his priestly association with the Temple of jerusalem. Under Mosiac law, the dove was declared to be pure. For this reason it was one of the few birds permitted as a sacrifice for purification after the birth of a child.

The dove also functions as a popular Marian symbol of purity, as does the vase of white lilies placed at the foot of the stairs. Further references to Mary are found in the assorted flowers growing in the immediate foreground. Forget-me-nots are often called "the eyes of Mary." Violets are symbolic of her humility, and daisies of her innocence. As stated by St. Bernard, Christ wished to be conceived "of a flower in the time of flowers."

In the distance, the city of Jerusalem can be seen. This corresponds to the location of the present Church of the Visitation in Ein Kerem, southwest of the Old City. The church is said to have been built over the house of John the Baptist's parents.

HAIL, MARY

Hail, Mary, full of grace, the Lord is with thee.
Blessed art thou among women
and blessed is the fruit of thy womb, Jesus.

Holy Mary, Mother of God. Pray for us sinners,
now and at the hour of our death. Amen.

HANNAH'S SONG OF PRAISE
(1 SAMUEL 2:1-10)

"My heart rejoices in the Lord;
in the Lord my horn is lifted high.
My mouth boasts over my enemies,
for I delight in your deliverance.
There is no one holy like the Lord;
there is no one besides you;
there is no Rock like our God.
Do not keep talking so proudly or
let your mouth speak such arrogance,
for the Lord is a God who knows,
and by him deeds are weighed.
The bows of the warriors are broken,
but those who stumbled are armed with strength.
Those who were full hire themselves out for food,
but those who were hungry hunger no more.
She who was barren has borne seven children,
but she who has had many sons pines away.
The Lord brings death and makes alive;
he brings down to the grave and raises up.
The Lord sends poverty and wealth;
he humbles and he exalts.
He raises the poor from the dust
and lifts the needy from the ash heap;
he seats them with princes and has
them inherit a throne of honor.
For the foundations of the earth are the Lord's;
upon them he has set the world.
He will guard the feet of his saints,
but the wicked will be silenced in darkness.

It is not by strength that one prevails;
those who oppose the Lord will be shattered.
He will thunder against them from heaven;
the Lord will judge the ends of the earth.
He will give strength to his king and exalt
the horn of his anointed."

A PRAYER OF SAINT TERESA OF AVILA

O God, have pity on so many perishing souls;
stay the course of so many evils which afflict
Christendom; and, without further delay,
cause Thy light to shine in the
midst of this darkness! Amen.

A PRAYER OF SAINT FRANCES XAVIER CABRINI

O God, fortify me with the grace of Your Holy Spirit
and give Your peace to my soul that I may be free
from all needless anxiety, solicitude, and worry.
Help me to desire always that which is pleasing
and acceptable to You so that
Your will may be my will. Amen.

"PRAYER FOR GENEROSITY" BY SAINT IGNATIUS OF LOYOLA

Teach us to be generous, good Lord;
teach us to serve You as You deserve;
to give and not to count the cost,
to fight and not to heed the wounds,
to toil and not to seek for rest,
to labor and not to ask for any reward
save that of knowing we do Your will. Amen.

A PRAYER OF SAINT CLAUDE DE LA COLOMBIERE

Lord, I am in this world to show Your mercy to others.
Other people will glorify You by making visible the power
of Your grace by their fidelity and constancy to You.
For my part, I will glorify You by making known how good
You are to sinners, that Your mercy is boundless

and that no sinner no matter how great his offenses
should have reason to despair of pardon.

If I have grievously offended You, My Redeemer,
let me not offend You even more by thinking that You
are not kind enough to pardon me. Amen.

PRAYER OF SAINT JOHN BOSCO TO " MARY, POWERFUL VIRGIN"

Mary, powerful Virgin, you are the mighty
and glorious protector of the Church.
You are the marvelous help of Christians.
You are awe-inspiring as an army in battle array.
You alone have destroyed every heresy in the whole world.

In the midst of our anguish, our struggle and our distress,
defend us from the power of the enemy, and at the
hour of our death receive our soul in heaven. Amen.

A PRAYER OF SAINT FRANCIS OF ASSISSI

Most high, glorious God, cast Your light into
the darkness of my heart.
Give me right faith, firm hope, perfect charity
and profound humility, with wisdom and perception,
O Lord, so that I may do what is truly
Your holy will. Amen.

"PEACE PRAYER" OF SAINT FRANCIS OF ASSISI

Lord, make me an instrument of Your peace;
where there is hatred, let me sow love;
where there is injury, pardon; where there is doubt, faith;
where there is despair, hope; where there is darkness,
light; and where there is sadness, joy.

Grant that I may not so much seek to be consoled as to console;
to be understood as to understand; to be loved as to love;
for it is in giving that we receive; it is in pardoning
that we are pardoned; and it is in dying that we are
born to eternal life. Amen.

"ON LOVE" BY SAINT THERESE OF LISIEUX

Miss no single opportunity of making some small sacrifice,
here by a smiling look, there by a kindly word;
always doing the smallest right and doing it all for love.

A PRAYER FOR PEACE OF MIND BY
SAINT FRANCES XAVIER CABRINI

Fortify me with the grace of Your Holy Spirit and give
Your peace to my soul that I may be free from
all needless anxiety, solicitude and worry.

Help me to desire always that which is pleasing
and acceptable to You so that Your will
may be my will. Amen.

A PRAYER OF SAINT ELIZABETH ANN SETON

O Father, the first rule of our dear
Saviour's life was to do Your Will.

Let His Will of the present moment be the first rule
of our daily life and work, with no other desire but
for its most full and complete accomplishment.
Help us to follow it faithfully, so that in doing
what You wish, we will be pleasing to You. Amen.

A PRAYER FOR FAITH AND PATIENCE

God, our Father, through the prayer of
Saint Rita, may we learn to bear our crosses
in life in the same spirit in which she bore hers.
And may we always recall her words that
"there is nothing impossible to God." Amen.

A PRAYER OF SAINT BONAVENTURE

O Mary, may my heart never cease to love you,
and my tongue never cease to praise you.

A PRAYER OF SAINT GERTRUDE

Most chaste Virgin Mary, I beg of you,
by that unspotted purity with which you prepared
for the Son of God a dwelling of delight
in your virginal womb, that by your intercession
I may be cleansed from every stain.

Most humble Virgin Mary, I beg of you,
by that most profound humility by which you deserved
to be raised high above all the choirs
of angels and saints, that by your intercession
all my sins may be expiated.

Most amiable Virgin Mary, I beg of you
by that unspeakable love which united you
so closely and inseparably to God,
that by your intercession I may obtain
an abundance of all merits. Amen.

A MARIAN PRAYER OF SAINT ILDEPHONSUS OF SPAIN

Virgin Mary, hear my prayer: through the Holy Spirit
you became the mother of Jesus;
from the Holy Spirit may I too have Jesus.

Through the Holy Spirit your flesh conceived Jesus;
through the same Holy Spirit may my soul receive Jesus.

Through the Holy Spirit you were able to know Jesus,
to possess Jesus, and to bring Him into the world.
Through the Holy Spirit may I too come to know your Jesus.

Imbued with the Spirit, Mary, you could say: "I am the handmaid
of the Lord, be it done to me according to your word";
in the Holy Spirit, lowly as I am, let me proclaim
the great truths about Jesus.

In the Spirit you now adore Jesus as Lord
and look on Him as Son; in the same spirit,
Mary, let me love your Jesus. Amen.

THE PRESENTATION OF JESUS IN THE TEMPLE
LUKE 2: 22-38
"THE PEOPLE WHO WALKED IN DARKNESS
HAVE SEEN A GREAT LIGHT"

"And when the time came for their purification according to the law of Moses, they brought him up to Jerusalem to present him to the Lord (as it is written in the law of the Lord, 'Every male that opens the womb shall be called holy to the Lord') and to offer a sacrifice according to what is said in the law of the Lord'"

In Jerusalem there lived a man, Simeon, who was just and devout. It had been revealed to him by the Holy Spirit that he would not die before he had seen the Lord's Christ. Led by the Holy Spirit into the Temple on the day that the Holy Family brought the Child Jesus to fulfill the law, Simeon took Jesus into his arms and blessed God, saying:

"'Lord, now lettest thou thy servant depart in peace, according to thy word; for mine eyes have seen thy salvation which thou hast prepared in the presence of all peoples, a light for revelation to the Gentiles, and for glory to thy people Israel.'"

Simeon blessed Mary and Joseph and spoke to Mary:

"'Behold, this child is set for the fall and rising of many in Israel, and for a sign that is spoken against (and a sword will pierce through your own soul, also), that thoughts out of many hearts may be revealed.'"

There was also a prophetess named Anna, who never left the Temple, but served God there by fasting and prayer. She came forward to Mary and Joseph and "gave thanks to God, and spoke of him to all who were looking for the redemption of Jerusalem."

"Shall I open the womb and not deliver? says the Lord" Isaiah 66:9

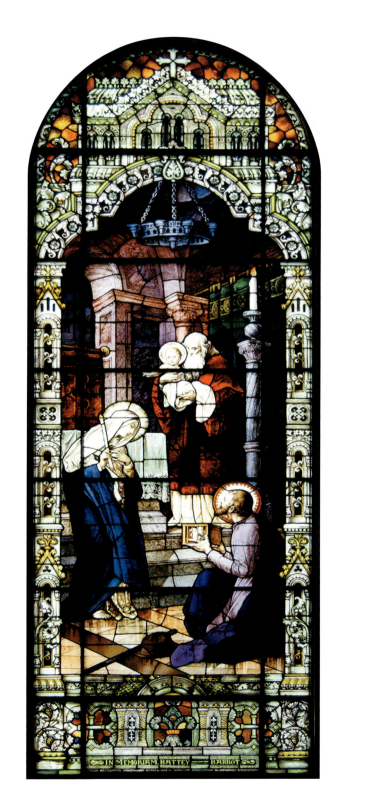

IN MEMORIAM. HATTEY   BARBOT

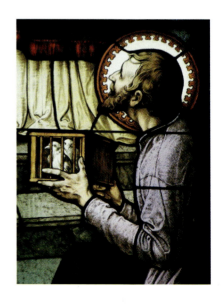

THE PURIFICATION OF MARY AND THE PRESENTATION OF CHRIST IN THE TEMPLE ICONOGRAPHY
Luke 2:22-24

According to the Mosaic law, a mother was required to go through a period of purification for the forty days after the birth of a male child (Leviticus 12:2,4). After the requisite number of days of purification had passed, she was to bring an offering to the Temple priest which would be offered before the Lord.

Mary and Joseph are depicted bringing the offering of two turtledoves, the offering of the poor, to the Temple for ceremonially cleansing: "And if she cannot afford a lamb, then she shall take two turtledoves or two young pigeons, one for a burnt offering and the other for a sin offering" (Leviticus 12:8).

This scene references both the *Presentation of Christ in the Temple* and the *Purification of the Virgin Mary*, which occurred at the same time. In accordance with the Law, all the firstborn in Israel were to be consecrated to the Lord (Exodus 13:2). As described in the Gospel: "And when the time came for their purification according to the law of Moses, they brought Him up to Jerusalem to present Him to the Lord ... and to offer a sacrifice according to what is said in the law of the Lord, 'a pair of turtledoves, or two young pigeons'" (Luke 2:22, 24). Joseph holds the two caged birds, the required offering for the Purification of Mary as well as that for the Presentation of Jesus.

Simeon, the "just and devout," is a significant figure in the Presentation narrative. The Holy Spirit had revealed to him that he would not die before he had seen the expected Messiah. Moved by the Spirit, he had gone into the Temple that day.

When Mary and Joseph brought their Child to the Temple, Simeon took Jesus, blessed God, and said: "Lord, now lettest thou thy servant depart in peace, according to thy word: for mine eyes have seen thy salvation which thou hast prepared in the presence of all peoples, a light for revelation to the Gentiles, and for glory to thy people Israel" (Luke 2:29-33). From the earliest times, light has symbolized the presence of God. The arrival of "the true light that gives light to every man" (John 1:9) was recognized by Simeon, and is wonderfully symbolized by his standing with the Christ Child between the lighted Christ candle and a lighted candle in Mary's hand, the latter signifying her role in bringing the Light into the world. The Temple lamp above them is unlit, indicating the "darkness" of the people of God before Christ enters. The prominence of the lighted candle held by Mary and the Christ candle directly refer to *Candlemas*, also known as the *Purification of the Virgin Mary* or the *Feast of the Presentation of Jesus in the Temple*

Simeon, who is placed opposite Mary and Joseph, stands slightly in front of and beside the altar dressed in priestly garments. Although he is not identified in the Scriptures as being of the priestly order, there is a long tradition of his being known as an "old priest," from the tribe of Aaron who worked in the Temple. In art, Simeon is always depicted wearing priestly robes.

Simeon is elevated above Mary and Joseph, standing on the top step, closest to the altar and lovingly cradling the Child, who is blessing His mother below Him. The Child has a tripartite halo, or nimbus. The three ornate bands prefigure the Crucifixion. The closeness of the Child to the altar also prefigures His sacrifice and reminds of Jesus' sacrificial presence on the altar.

Simeon and the Child Jesus direct their attention downward to the Blessed Virgin, whose figure dominates the scene. Her dress is the same as that in the Visitation window. Her ornately embroidered white and gold gown emphasizes her purity. She elegantly poses with her head humbly bowed, holding a lighted candle in her right hand. Her nimbus, or halo, is the starred crown based upon the description in Revelation 12:1.

Joseph's attention is also directed toward Mary as he kneels with the two caged turtledoves. His simple yet identifiable hat and staff are on the floor beside him, alluding to the distance Joseph and Mary had traveled from Bethlehem to Jerusalem and prefiguring the flight into Egypt.

THE NUNC DIMITTIS

Lord, now You let Your servant go in peace;
Your word has been fulfilled.
My eyes have seen the salvation
You have prepared in the sight of every people,
a light to reveal You to the nations
and the glory of Your people, Israel.

A PRAYER OF SAINT BENEDICT OF NURSIA

Father, in Your goodness grant me the intellect
to comprehend You, the perception to discern
You, and the reason to appreciate You.
In Your kindness endow me with the diligence
to look for You, the wisdom to discover You,
and the spirit to apprehend You.
In Your graciousness bestow on me a heart
to contemplate You, ears to hear You,
eyes to see You, and a tongue to speak of You.
In Your mercy confer on me a conversation pleasing
to You, the patience to wait for You, and
the perseverance to long for You.
Grant me a perfect end - Your holy presence. Amen.

THE BLESSED MOTHER TERESA OF CALCUTTA'S DAILY PRAYER, WRITTEN BY JOHN HENRY CARDINAL NEWMAN

Dear Jesus, Help me to spread Thy
fragrance everywhere I go.
Flood my soul with Thy spirit and love.
Penetrate and possess my whole being so utterly
that all my life may only be a radiance of Thine.

Shine through me and be so in me that every soul I come
in contact with may feel Thy presence in my soul.
Let them look up and see no longer me but only Jesus.

Stay with me and then I shall begin to shine as
You shine, so to shine as to be a light to others.
The light, O Lord, will be all from You; none of it will be

mine; it will be You shining on others through me.
Let me thus praise You in the way You love best,
by shining on those around me.

Let me preach You without preaching, not by words
but by my example, by the catching force, the
sympathetic influence of what I do, the evident
fullness of the love my heart bears to You. Amen.

PRAYER OF SAINT AMBROSE OF MILAN THAT WE MAY SEEK GOD AND FIND HIM

Lord, teach me to seek You, and reveal
Yourself to me when I seek You.
For I cannot seek You unless You first teach me,
nor find You unless You first reveal Yourself to me.
Let me seek You in longing and long for You in seeking.
Let me find You in love, and love You in finding. Amen.

A PRAYER OF THE VENERABLE BEDE

O Christ, our Morning Star, Splendor of Light Eternal,
shining with the glory of the rainbow,
come and waken us from the grayness of our
apathy and renew in us Your gift of hope.
Bring me into Your presence
that I may listen to Your voice,
which is the source of all wisdom,
and gaze upon Your face forever. Amen.

PRAYER TO MARY

Mary, most sorrowful, Mother of Christians, pray for us. Amen.

THE LORD'S PRAYER

Our Father, Who art in heaven, hallowed be Thy name.
Thy kingdom come; Thy will be done on earth as it is in heaven.
Give us this day our daily bread; and forgive us our
trespasses as we forgive those who trespass against us.
Lead us not into temptation, but deliver us from evil. Amen.

THE VIA MATRIS

I. THE PROPHECY OF SIMEON
Reflect on the sorrow of Our Blessed Lady, when she presented her Divine Child in the temple and heard from the aged Simeon that a sword of grief should pierce her soul.

II. THE FLIGHT INTO EGYPT
Reflect on her sorrow when, to escape the cruelty of King Herod, she was forced to fly into Egypt with Saint Joseph and her beloved Child.

III. THE LOSS OF JESUS IN THE TEMPLE
Reflect on her grief when, in returning to Jerusalem, she found that she had lost her dear Jesus Whom she sought sorrowing for three days.

IV. MARY MEETS JESUS ON THE WAY
Reflect on her meeting her Divine Son, all bruised and bleeding, carrying His Cross to Calvary, and seeing Him fall under its heavy weight.

V. JESUS DIES ON THE CROSS
Reflect on her standing by when her Divine Son was lifted up on the Cross and the blood flowed in streams from His Sacred Wounds.

VI. MARY RECEIVES THE DEAD BODY OF JESUS
Reflect on her sorrow when Her Divine Son was taken down from the Cross and placed in her arms.

VII. JESUS IS PLACED IN THE TOMB
Reflect on her following His Sacred Body as it was borne by Joseph of Arimathea and Nicodemus to the sepulcher.

After meditating on the Seven Sorrows of Mary, recite three Hail Mary's in honor of Our Blessed Lady's tears.

TANTUM ERGO

Tantum ergo Sacramentum
Veneremur cernui:
Et antiquum documentum
Novo cedat ritui:

Praestet fides supplementum
Sensuum defectui.

Genitori, Genitoque
Laus et iubilatio,
Salus, honor, virtus quoque
Sit et benedictio:
Precedenti ab utroque
Compar sit laudatio. Amen.

PRAYER OF POPE CLEMENT XI

I pray, Lord, that You enlighten my mind, inflame my
will, purify my heart, and sanctify my soul. Amen

A PRAYER BY SAINT IGNATIUS OF LOYOLA

Jesus, fill us, we pray, with Your light and life
that we may show forth Your wonderful glory.
Grant that Your love may so fill our lives that
we may count nothing too small to do for You,
nothing too much to give, and
nothing too hard to bear. Amen.

A PRAYER OF SAINT PETER OF ALCANTARA

Hear me, O Lord, my soul's delight, joy of my heart,
not because of my merits, but because of Your boundless goodness.

Teach me, enlighten me, direct me; help me in all things,
that I may never say or do anything but what I know
to be pleasing in Your sight.

Guide me, O God, my love, my light, and my life. Amen.

THE FLIGHT INTO EGYPT
"OUT OF EGYPT HAVE I CALLED MY SON"

The night Jesus was born, magi in the East saw the special star in the sky. They journeyed to Jerusalem to find the newborn king of the Jews. The chief priests and scribes directed the magi on to Bethlehem, but they themselves stayed behind in Jerusalem. After the magi found Mary, Joseph and the young Child in a house, they worshiped the Child and then returned to their own country.

"When they had departed, behold, an angel of the Lord appeared to Joseph in a dream and said, 'Rise, take the child and his mother, and flee to Egypt, and remain there till I tell you; for Herod is about to search for the child, to destroy him.' And he rose and took the child and his mother by night, and departed for Egypt" (Matthew 2: 13-14).

Herod soon learned that the magi had left the country, foiling his plan to use them to locate the threat to his kingdom. He was furious. Herod acted swiftly to kill the young king.

"He sent and killed all the male children in Bethlehem and in all that region who were two years old or under, according to the time which he had ascertained from the wise men. Then was fulfilled what was spoken by the prophet Jeremiah: 'A voice was heard in Ramah, wailing and loud lamentation, Rachel weeping for her children; she refused to be consoled, because they were no more'" (Matthew 2:16-18).

Joseph kept Jesus and Mary in Egypt until he was told by an angel in a dream that Herod was dead and it was safe to return to the land of Israel. Then, he took his family to Nazareth.

The angel of the Lord appeared to Joseph in dreams on three or possibly four occasions. Each time Joseph responded faithfully and without question in accordance with God's commands. May we also be obedient to the will of the Lord.

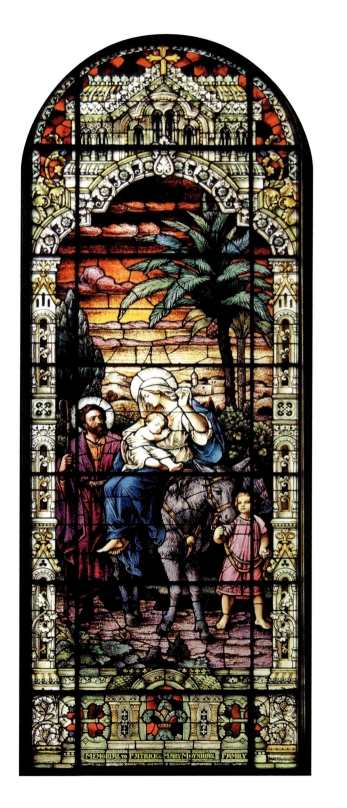

MEMORIAL TO PATRICK & MARY MOYNIHAN FAMILY

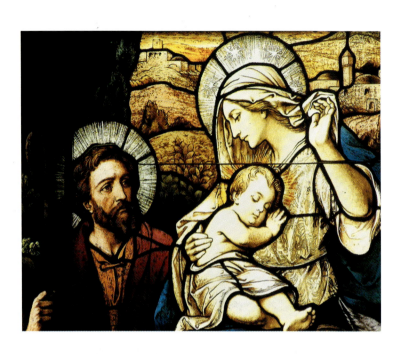

THE FLIGHT INTO EGYPT ICONOGRAPHY
Matthew 2:13-15

When Herod the Great heard that a Child had been born who would become King of the Jews, he decreed the killing of all male children in Bethlehem who were two years of age and under (the Slaughter of the Innocents). An angel appeared to Joseph in a dream, warning him to take the Infant Jesus and escape into Egypt. Joseph was instructed to stay there until he was told to return to Israel, because Herod would search for the Child to kill him (Matthew 2:13-14). Joseph followed these instructions and took Jesus and Mary by night, fleeing to Egypt where they stayed until the death of Herod. The scene depicting the journey of the Holy Family is termed the "Flight into Egypt."

Over the centuries Matthew's simple account of the flight became a popular subject for artists. A complex iconography gradually emerged drawn on descriptions from the apocryphal gospels. The Franz Mayer window closely resembles a painting by a nineteenth-century German artist and professor, Bernard Plockhörst (1825-1907), whose religious paintings were widely copied and distributed.

Plockhörst, as does the Mayer artist, depicts Mary riding sidesaddle on a gray donkey while the Christ Child sleeps peacefully on her lap. She is dressed in a white robe and veil with a blue mantle. She uses her mantle as a protective wrap which she gently lifts, enabling the viewer to gaze upon the radiant head of Christ. Mary is crowned with the star nimbus that she wears in all but one of the Mayer windows.

The artist deviates from Matthew's account by including a young angel with purple wings who holds the halter of the donkey, safely leading the Holy Family on their arduous journey. Identified by his familiar yellow tunic and staff, Joseph takes up the rear guard, being ever steadfast in his role as guardian and protector of Mary and the Christ Child.

The cityscape of Bethlehem located in the far distance of the background indicates that they are well along on their journey. The palm trees located on the right assist in identifying the eastern landscape. The palms also reference an excerpt from the Gospel of Pseudo-Matthew that often was included in paintings of this subject. The legend describes how along the journey a palm tree miraculously bent downward so that the Holy Family was nourished by its fruit and refreshed by a gush of water that sprang forth from its roots.

"A PRAYER FOR LIFE" BY POPE BLESSED JOHN PAUL II

O Mary, bright dawn of the new world, Mother of the living, to you do we entrust the cause of life:

Look down, O Mother, upon the vast numbers of babies not allowed to be born, upon the poor whose lives are made difficult, upon men and women who are victims of brutal violence, upon the elderly and the sick killed by indifference or out of misguided mercy.

Grant that all who believe in your Son may proclaim the Gospel of life with honesty and love to the people of our time.

Obtain for them the grace to accept that Gospel as a gift ever new, the joy of celebrating it with gratitude throughout their lives, and the courage to bear witness to it resolutely, in order to build, together with all people of good will, the civilization of truth and love, to the praise and glory of God, the Creator and lover of life. Amen.

PRAYER TO SAINT MICHAEL THE ARCHANGEL

Saint Michael the Archangel, defend us in battle. Be our defense against the wickedness and snares of the Devil. May God rebuke him, we humbly pray; and do thou, O prince of the heavenly host, by the power of God, cast into hell Satan and all the evil spirits who prowl about the world seeking the ruin of souls. Amen.

A PRAYER OF SAINT CYPRIAN OF CARTHAGE

Good God, may we confess Your Name to the end; may we emerge unmarked and glorious from the traps and darkness of this world. As You have bound us together by charity and peace, and as together we have persevered under persecution, so may we also rejoice together in Your heavenly kingdom. Amen.

A PRAYER OF SAINT TERESA OF AVILA

Let nothing disturb thee; Let nothing dismay thee;
All things pass; God never changes.
Patience attains all that it strives for.
He who has God finds he lacks for nothing:
God alone suffices. Amen.

A PRAYER OF ARCHBISHOP FULTON J. SHEEN

Jesus, Mary, and Joseph, I love you very much.
I beg you to spare the life of the unborn baby that I have
spiritually adopted who is in danger of abortion. Amen.

TRINITY PRAYER

Love of Jesus, fill us.
Holy Spirit, guide us.
Will of the Father be done. Amen.

"A PRAYER TO THE GUARDIAN ANGEL" BY SAINT PIO OF PIETRELCINA

Angel of God, my guardian, to whom the goodness
of the Heavenly Father entrusts me.
Enlighten, protect and guide me now and forever. Amen.

A PRAYER TO END ABORTION

Heavenly Father, have mercy on our nation and the world.
Through the light and truth of Your Spirit, return our
society to a system of justice that holds all life sacred.
I pray for the children who today will be returned
to You by the martyrdom of abortion.
May the sufferings and blood of these holy innocents
be united with the Most Precious Blood of
the Lamb, Who won for us salvation.
May they obtain through You, Author of all life,
an end to the slaughter throughout the world.
In the most powerful Name of Your Son,
our Lord Jesus Christ. Amen.

PRAYER TO MARY, MOTHER OF THE LIFE WITHIN

O Mary, Mother of the Life Within, all life we entrust to you:
The life of every expectant mother and the child within her womb;
the life of every human body and the life of every human soul; the
life of every newborn child and the life of all grown old.

You held the Lord to your own heart and drew Him
closely in to you. So draw us now to you.
For all our needs, O Mother of the Life Within,
pray for us. Amen.

A PRAYER FOR THE SANCTITY OF LIFE

Father and Maker of all, You adorn all creation
with splendor and beauty, and fashion human
lives in Your image and likeness.
Awaken in every heart reverence for the work of
Your hands, and renew among Your people a readiness
to nurture and sustain Your precious gift of life.
Grant this through our Lord Jesus Christ,
Your Son, who lives and reigns with You in the unity
of the Holy Spirit, God forever and ever. Amen.

A PRAYER BY SAINT PIO OF PIETRELCINA

May Jesus comfort you in all your afflictions.
May He sustain you in dangers, watch over you
always with His grace, and indicate the safe
path that leads to eternal salvation.
And may He render you always dearer to His
Divine Heart and always more worthy of Paradise. Amen.

A MEDITATION OF SAINT ALPHONSUS LIGOURI

It often happens that we pray to God to deliver us from
some dangerous temptation, and yet God does not
hear us but permits the temptation to continue troubling us.
In such a case, let us understand that God permits
even this for our greater good.

When a soul in temptation recommends itself to God,
and by His aid resists, O how it then
advances in perfection.

"BE AT PEACE" BY SAINT FRANCIS DE SALES

Do not look forward in fear to the changes in life;
rather, look to them with full hope that as they arise,
God, whose very own you are, will lead you safely
through all things; and when you cannot stand it,
God will carry you in His arms.
Do not fear what may happen tomorrow; the same
understanding Father who cares for you today will
take care of you then and every day.
He will either shield you from suffering
or will give you unfailing strength to bear it.
Be at peace, and put aside
all anxious thoughts and imaginations.

A PRAYER OF SAINT COLUMBA OF IRELAND

O Lord, grant us that love which can never die,
which will enkindle our lamps but not extinguish
them, so that they may shine in us
and bring light to others.
Most dear Saviour, enkindle our lamps that
they may shine forever in Your temple.
May we receive unquenchable light from You so that
our darkness will be illuminated and the darkness
of the world will be made less. Amen.

A PRAYER OF SAINT AUGUSTINE OF HIPPO

Watch, O Lord, with those who wake, or
watch, or weep tonight, and give Your Angels
and Saints charge over those who sleep.
Tend Your sick one, O Lord Christ.
Rest Your weary ones. Bless Your dying ones.
Soothe Your suffering ones.
Pity Your afflicted ones. Shield Your joyous ones.
And all for Your love's sake. Amen.

A PRAYER BY BLESSED MOTHER TERESA OF CALCUTTA

Lord, increase my faith, bless my efforts
and work, now and for evermore. Amen.

PRAYER OF SAINT PATRICK FOR THE FAITHFUL

May the Strength of God guide us.
May the Power of God preserve us.
May the Wisdom of God instruct us.
May the Hand of God protect us.
May the Way of God direct us.
May the Shield of God defend us.
May the Angels of God guard us,
against the snares of the evil one.

May Christ be with us! May Christ be before us!
May Christ be in us, Christ over all!

May Thy Grace, Lord, always be ours,
this day, O Lord, and forevermore. Amen.

PRAYER OF POPE BLESSED JOHN PAUL II

Mother of the Church, grant that the Church may
enjoy freedom and peace in fulfilling her saving mission
and that to this end she may become mature with a
new maturity of faith and inner unity.

Help us to overcome opposition and difficulties.
Help us to rediscover all the simplicity and
dignity of the Christian vocation.
Grant that there may be no lack of
"laborers in the Lord's vineyard."
Sanctify families. Watch over the souls of the
young and the hearts of the children.
Help us to overcome the great moral threats
against the fundamental spheres of life and love.
Obtain for us the grace to be continually renewed
through all the beauty of witness given to
the cross and resurrection of your Son. Amen.

THE WEDDING FEAST AT CANA
JESUS' FIRST MIRACLE
JOHN 2:1-11
"DO WHATEVER HE TELLS YOU TO DO."

"On the third day there was a marriage at Cana in Galilee, and the mother of Jesus was there; Jesus also was invited to the marriage , with his disciples. When the wine failed, the mother of Jesus said to him, 'They have no wine.' And Jesus said to her, 'O woman, what have you to do with me? My hour has not yet come.' His mother said to the servants, 'Do whatever he tells you.'"

Our Lady's words can be seen as a permanent invitation to each of us. Saint Thomas Aquinas states that "in [these words of Our Lady] all Christian holiness consists: for perfect holiness is obeying Christ in all things" (St. Thomas Aquinas, Commentary On St. John).

"Now six stone jars were standing there, for the Jewish rites of purification, each holding twenty or thirty gallons. Jesus said to them, 'Fill the jars with water'. And they filled them up to the brim. He sais to them, 'Now draw some out, and take it to the steward of the feast.' So they took it."

The servants knew what they were asked to do by Jesus. They could have questioned Jesus, made suggestions, decided they had a better plan, left the task to others, halfheartedly complied, or refused. Instead, they followed Our Lady's advice and did what Jesus asked. He told them to fill the jars with water and they filled the jars to the brim.

"When the steward of the feast tasted the water now become wine, and did not know where it came from (though the servants who had drawn the water knew), the steward of the feast called the bridegroom and said to him, 'Every man serves the good wine first; and when men have drunk freely, then the poor wine; but you have kept the good wine until now.'"

"Serve God. He will take care of the results" (St. Therese of Lisieux). Trust and obey and God will do the rest.

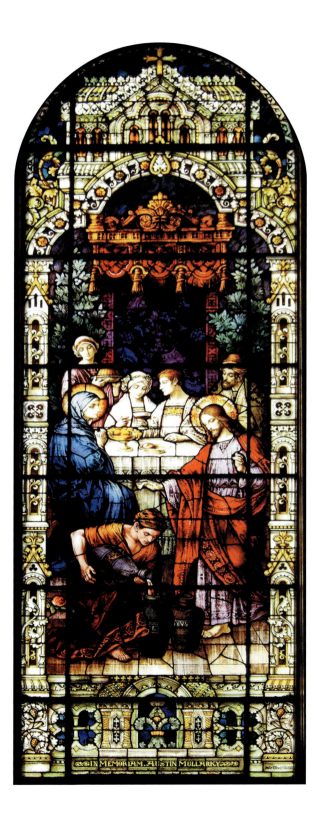

IN MEMORIAM AUSTIN MULLARKY

THE WEDDING FEAST AT CANA ICONOGRAPHY
John 2:1-11

The first public miracle performed by Christ, recorded only in the Gospel of John, was at a wedding in the town of Cana in Galilee. This window depicts the wedding feast taking place in an open stone courtyard, where the bride and groom are seated at the table of honor. They are centrally placed in front of an ornately embroidered fabric canopy, fringed with gold tassels, and flanked by fruit-bearing trees. The young couple, dressed primarily in white, which is the color of purity, is enjoying the wine and fruit before them as servers enter from both sides bearing foods for the celebration.

Prior to the moment captured in the window tableau, Jesus, informed by His mother that the wine had run out, has instructed the servants to "fill the jars with water" (John 2:7). The Mayer artist shows in the left forefront of the window a male servant, arrayed in a rich damask garment, pouring water into an earthenware jar. Jesus stands to the right, behind the servant, but in front of the wedding table. He is dressed in a purple robe with a red cloak with His right hand raised over the servant and jar. Jesus' head is surrounded by an elaborate nimbus, or halo, with the triple division symbolizing the Trinity. Miraculously, as the clear water flows into each stone jar, it turns into a fine red wine.

Seated in front of the table, Mary, dressed in a blue robe and mantle with the star nimbus surrounding her head, sits quietly with her hands clasped in front of her. She appears to be reflecting on the miracle unfolding before her and the revelation of her Son's glory.

From at least the fourth century, depictions of the Marriage at Cana were intended to be seen as a prefiguration of the Eucharist. At the heart of the Eucharistic celebration are the bread and wine, both of which figure prominently in this scene. A single loaf of bread lies on a golden platter in front of the bridal couple, while the groom holds a chalice of wine that is strategically placed directly over the bread. These items are part of an implied vertical axis that, continuing downward, intersects through the extended right hand of Christ and the vase of newly-poured wine. Through the changing of the bread and wine into Christ's body and blood, Christ becomes present in the Eucharist, 'the bread of heaven' and 'the cup of salvation.'

Lying on the step in front of Mary, and just behind the servant filling the stone jars, is a single red rose. The rose is one of the principal symbols of the Virgin who, being free of original sin, has long been called the 'rose without a thorn.' However, a red rose also symbolizes martyrdom or blood, and is intended in this context, along with the jars of wine, to allude to the sacrificial character of the Eucharist.

Pope John Paul II frequently spoke of the nuptial character of the Eucharist and its special relationship with the sacrament of Matrimony: "The Eucharist is the sacrament of our redemption. It is the sacrament of the Bridegroom and of the Bride" (Apostolic Letter *Mulieris Dignitatem*, 1988). The artist of this scene has masterfully rendered a literal depiction of the Marriage at Cana and has at the same time symbolized the intrinsic relationship existing between the sacraments of Matrimony and the Eucharist. Saint Paul states: "Husbands, love your wives, as Christ loved the church and gave himself up for her ..." (Ephesians 5:25).

THE JESUS PRAYER OF SAINT JOHN GABRIEL PERBOYRE

O my Divine Saviour, transform me into Yourself.
May my hands be the hands of Jesus.
May my tongue be the tongue of Jesus.

Grant that every faculty of my body
may serve only to glorify You.
Above all, transform my soul and all its powers,
so that my memory, my will and my affections
may be the memory, the will and the affections of Jesus.

I pray You to destroy in me all that is not You.
Grant that I may live but in You and for You,
and that I may truly say with St. Paul:
"I live, now not I, but Christ lives in me" (Gal. 2:20).

A PRAYER FOR THE HOME

We beseech You, O Lord,
visit this home, and drive from it
all the snares of the enemy;
let Your holy angels dwell herein
so as to preserve us in peace;
and let Your blessing be always upon us.
Through Christ, our Lord, Amen.

AN ASPIRATION TO JESUS

Good Jesus, give me a deep love for You,
that nothing may be too hard for me
to bear from You.
Jesus, I trust in You! Amen.

PRAYER FROM THE GELASIAN SACRAMENTARY (c.750)

Almighty and everlasting God, be present with us in
all our duties, and grant the protection of Your
presence to all that dwell in this house, that You may
be known to be the Defender of this household
and the Inhabitant of this dwelling. Amen.

A PRAYER OF SAINT THOMAS AQUINAS

Almighty and everlasting God, behold I come
to the Sacrament of Thine only-begotten
Son, our Lord Jesus Christ. I come as
one infirm to the physician of life,
as one unclean to the fountain of mercy,
as one blind to the light of everlasting brightness,
as one poor and needy to the Lord of heaven and earth.

Therefore I implore the abundance of
Thy measureless bounty that Thou wouldst vouchsafe
to heal my infirmity, wash my uncleanness,
enlighten my blindness, enrich my poverty and
clothe my nakedness, that I may receive the
Bread of Angels, the King of kings, the Lord of lords,
with such reverence and humility,
with such sorrow and devotion, with such purity and
faith, with such purpose and intention
as may be profitable to my soul's salvation.

Grant unto me, I pray, the grace of receiving not
only the Sacrament of our Lord's Body and Blood,
but also the grace and power of the Sacrament.

O most gracious God, grant me so to receive
the Body of Thine only-begotten Son,
our Lord Jesus Christ, which He took from the Virgin Mary,
as to merit to be incorporated into His mystical Body,
and to be numbered amongst His members.

O most loving Father, give me grace to behold
forever Thy beloved Son with His face at last unveiled,
whom I now purpose to receive under the
sacramental veil here below. Amen.

THE MIRACLE PRAYER

Lord Jesus, I come before You just as I am.
I am sorry for my sins; I repent of my sins; please forgive me.
In Your name, I forgive all others for what

they have done against me.
I renounce Satan, the evil spirits and all their works.
I give You my entire self.
Lord Jesus, now and forever, I invite You into my life.
Jesus, I accept You as my Lord and Saviour.
Heal me; change me; strengthen me in body, soul and spirit.

Come, Lord Jesus, cover me with Your precious Blood
and fill me with Your Holy Spirit.
I love You, Jesus.
I praise You, Jesus.
I thank You, Jesus.
I shall follow You every day of my life. Amen.

A PRAYER OF CHRISTINA ROSSETTI

Grant us such grace that we may
work Your will and speak Your words,
and walk before Your face, profound
and calm like waters deep and still;
Grant us such grace. Amen.

A PRAYER OF SAINT VINCENT FERRER FOR A HAPPY DEATH

Lord Jesus Christ, who willest that no man
should perish, and to whom supplication
is never made without hope of mercy,
for Thou saidst with Thine
own holy and blessed lips:
"All things whatsoever ye shall ask
in My name, shall be done unto you";

I ask of Thee, O Lord, for Thy holy Name's sake,
to grant me at the hour of my death
full consciousness and the power of speech,
sincere contrition for my sins,
true faith, firm hope, and perfect charity, that
I may be able to say unto Thee with a clean heart:
Into Thy hands, O Lord, I commend my spirit:
Thou hast redeemed me, O God of truth,
Who art blessed for ever and ever. Amen.

VENI CREATOR SPIRITUS

Come, O Creator Spirit blest!
And in our souls take up Thy rest;
Come with Thy grace and heavenly aid,
To fill the hearts which Thou hast made.
Great Paraclete! To Thee we cry,
O highest gift of God most high!
O font of life! O fire of love!
And sweet anointing from above.

Thou in Thy sevenfold gifts art known,
The finger of God's hand we own;
The promise of the Father, Thou!
Who dost the tongue with power endow.

Kindle our senses from above,
And make our hearts overflow with love;

With patience firm and virtue high
The weakness of our flesh supply.

Far from us drive the foe we dread,
And grant us Thy true peace instead;

So shall we not, with Thee for guide,
Turn from the path of life aside.

O, may Thy grace on us bestow
The Father and the Son to know,
And Thee, through endless times confessed,
Of both, the eternal Spirit blest.

All glory while the ages run
Be to the Father and the Son
Who rose from death; the same to Thee,
O Holy Ghost, eternally. Amen.

SACRED HEART OF JESUS

Sacred Heart of Jesus, Thy kingdom come! Amen.

PANGE LINGUA

Pange lingua gloriosi
corporis mysterium,
sanguinisque pretiosi,
quem in mundi pretium
fructus ventris generosi,
rex effudit gentium.

Nobis datus, nobis natus
ex intacta Virgine
et in mundo conversatus,
sparso verbi semine,
sui moras incolatus
miro clausit ordine.

In supremae nocte coenae
recumbens cum fratribus,
observata lege plene
cibis turbae duodenae
se dat suis manibus.

Verum caro, panem verum
verbo carnem efficit:
fitque sanguis Christi merum,
et si sensus deficit,
ad firmandum cor sincerum
sola fides sufficit. Amen.

O SAVING VICTIM

O Saving Victim, op'ning wide
The gate of heav'n to us below!
Our foes press on from ev'ry side:
Your aid supply, Your strength bestow.

To Your great name be endless praise,
Immortal Godhead, One in Three;
O grant us endless length of days
When our true native land we see.

JESUS BLESSES THE CHILDREN
MATTHEW 19:13-15; MARK 10:13-16; LUKE 18:15-17
"LET THE CHILDREN COME TO ME, DO NOT HINDER THEM"

"Then children were brought to him that he might lay his hands on them and pray" (Matthew 19:13).

The children were being brought to Jesus. They were too young to come to him by themselves. The Gospel of Luke makes it even clearer: *"they were bringing even infants."* The "they" in all three Gospel references is not limited to parents or relatives. God lays the duty on all to bring the young to Him.

The disciples' reaction to the eager grown-ups' bringing the children to Jesus was to *"rebuke them."* It seemed obvious that Jesus had more important things to do than waste time over babies and children.

Jesus did not agree: *"But when Jesus saw it he was indignant" (Mark 10:14).* There are few times in the Bible when Jesus loses patience with His disciples and this is one of them. Usually, Jesus gently corrects their wrongheaded thinking. Jesus, however, is extremely protective of children. When the disciples try to block access of the children to God, Jesus becomes "indignant." Matt: 18:5-6; Mark 9:42; Luke 17:1-2.

"Let the children come to me, do not hinder them...." Mark 10:14. We are to remove all hindrances - all spiritual or physical roadblocks - that keep children from coming to Jesus.

Jesus blessed the children after explaining to the disciples that *"to such belongs the kingdom of God" (Mark 10:14).*What are those special qualifications. Perhaps it is a combination of what a child lacks - achievements, accomplishments, independent self-reliance.
"Train up a child in the way he should go, and when he is old he will not depart from it." Proverb 22:6

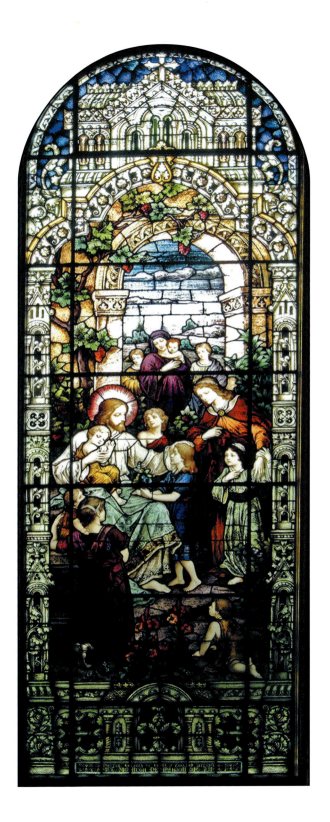

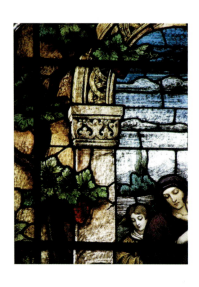

JESUS BLESSES THE CHILDREN ICONOGRAPHY
Matthew 19:13-14; Mark 10:13-16; Luke 18:15-17

Sitting in a pastoral garden setting overflowing with an abundance of colorful flowers and green bushes, Jesus affectionately welcomes a small crowd of children as they gather around Him. One sits contentedly in Jesus' embrace while another adoringly presents a bouquet of freshly picked wild flowers. The lilies of the valley, daisies and blue flowers are all associated with innocence, chastity, and humility. The children's trust and devotion to Jesus is apparent in their solemn attention to Him. Accompanied or carried by their mothers, children of all ages come close to eagerly receive His Blessing. The disciples who had attempted to keep the children from Jesus are not depicted in the window. The walls of the city of Jerusalem can be seen in the background.

The scene is closely modeled after a popular painting by the German artist Heinrich Hofmann (1824-1902), whose works were widely distributed and subsequently adapted into stained glass. Hofmann's charming figural types, with their child-like appearances, were borrowed by the Mayer artist and placed within an idealized natural setting. The essence of tenderness and compassion has been achieved.

The Mayer artist has made alterations to the Hofmann composition, adding an assortment of finely detailed flowers, plants and bushes. A climbing grape vine adorns the stone wall behind Jesus and extends upward along the arched doorway. Heavily laden with clusters of red grapes, the vine serves as a compositional device to accentuate the figure of Christ, prefiguring His sacrifice and the institution of the Eucharist.

An abundant vine is also used in Scripture as a symbol of Israel and to express the relationship between God and His people. Sometimes it implies a vineyard, a protected place where the

-109-

children of God, the vines, flourish under the care of God, the keeper of the vineyard (Isaiah 65:21-22). The vine also serves as a symbol of Christ who states: "I am the true vine, and my Father is the vinegrower...I am the vine, you are the branches. Those who abide in me and I in them bear much fruit, because apart from me you can do nothing" (John 15:1, 5).

Jesus is wearing a white robe with a fleur-de-lis pattern adorning the sleeves and hem, and the pale blue mantle around His waist and lap is woven with a cross and shamrock pattern. The shamrock points to the Trinity as well as to Saint Patrick, one of the patron saints of the parish. According to tradition, Saint Patrick used the shamrock to illustrate the concept of the Trinity.

Jesus is depicted in the window scene freely giving the blessings of the kingdom to those who, like children, are prepared to receive these blessings as a gift of God. God in turn is glorified in the fruit-bearing of his followers.

A PRAYER OF SAINT IRENAEUS OF LYONS

Father, give perfection to beginners, understanding
to the little ones, and help to those
who are running their course.
Give sorrow to the negligent, fervor to
the lukewarm, and a good consummation
to the perfect. Amen.

A PRAYER OF POPE SAINT LEO THE GREAT

Make us peacemakers, O God, that we may be
called children of God and joint heirs with Christ.
May we never suffer calamities, never fear temptation.

When the struggle is over, may we rest in the peace
of God, the peace of utter tranquillity, through
our Lord, who with the Father and the Holy Spirit
lives and reigns forever and ever. Amen.

A MORNING OFFERING

O Jesus, I offer You all the prayers, thoughts,
works and sufferings of this day.
Grant, O Lord, that no one may love
You less this day because of me; that no word
or action of mine may turn a soul from You,
and that many souls will love You more this day
because of me. Amen.

A PRAYER OF SAINT TERESA OF AVILA

Lord, grant that I may always allow myself
to be guided by You, always follow Your plans,
and perfectly accomplish Your holy will.
Grant that in all things, great and small,
today and all the days of my life, I may do
whatever You may require of me.
Help me to respond to the slightest promptings
of Your grace, so that I may be

Your trustworthy instrument, for Your honor.
May Your will be done in time and eternity -
by me, in me, and through me. Amen.

HAIL, QUEEN OF HEAVEN

Hail, Queen of heav'n, the ocean star,
guide of the wand'rer here below:
thrown on life's surge, we claim thy care;
save us from peril and from woe.
Mother of Christ, star of the sea,
pray for the wand'rer, pray for me.

O gentle, chaste and spotless maid,
we sinners make our pray through thee;
remind thy son that He has paid
the price of our iniquity.
Virgin most pure, star of the sea,
pray for the sinner, pray for me.

Sojourners in this vale of tears,
to thee, blest advocate, we cry:
pity our sorrows, calm our fears,
and soothe with hope our misery.
Refuge in grief, star of the sea,
pray for the mourner, pray for me.

And while to Him who reigns above,
in Godhead One, in Persons Three,
the source of life, of grace, of love,
homage we pay on bended knee,
do thou, bright Queen, star of the sea,
pray for the children, pray for me.

A CHILD'S PRAYER FOR PROTECTION

Angel of God, my Guardian dear,
to whom God's love commits me here;
ever this day be at my side
to light and guard,
to rule and guide. Amen.

MARY, MOTHER OF GRACE

Mary, Mother of grace, Mother of mercy,
shield me from the enemy and
receive me at the hour of my death. Amen.

A PRAYER OF SAINT RICHARD OF CHICHESTER

Thanks be to Thee, my Lord Jesus Christ,
for the benefits Thou hast given me, for all
the pains and insults Thou hast borne for me.

O most merciful Redeemer, Friend, and Brother,
may I know Thee more clearly, love Thee more dearly,
and follow Thee more nearly, day by day. Amen.

HAIL MARY, GENTLE WOMAN

Gentle woman, quiet light,
morning star so strong and bright,
gentle mother, peaceful dove,
teach us wisdom, teach us love.

You were chosen by the Father,
you were chosen for the Son,
you were chosen from all women
and for woman shining one.

Blessed are you among women,
blessed in turn all women, too,
blessed they with peaceful spirits,
blessed they with gentle hearts. Amen.

SUSCIPE, A PRAYER OF SAINT IGNATIUS LOYOLA

Take, Lord, and receive all my liberty,
my memory, my understanding and my entire will.
All I have and call my own.
You have given it all to me.
To You, Lord, I return it.
Everything is Yours; do with it as You will.

Give me only Your love and Your grace.
That is enough for me. Amen.

FOR MOTHER WITH CHILD

O almighty and everlasting God, through the Holy Spirit,
You prepared the body and soul of the glorious virgin Mary
to be a worthy dwelling place of Your divine Son.

Through the same Holy Spirit, You sanctified
Saint John the Baptist, while still in his mother's womb.

Hear the prayers of your humble servant who
implores You, through the intercession of St. Gerard,
to protect me amid the dangers of childbearing
and to watch over the child which with You blessed me.

May this child be cleansed by the saving water of
baptism and, after a Christian life on earth,
may we, both mother and child, attain
everlasting bliss in heaven. Amen.

A PRAYER OF POPE SAINT CLEMENT OF ROME

O God almighty, Father of our Lord Jesus Christ,
grant us to be grounded and settled in Your truth
by the coming down of the Holy Spirit into our hearts.

That which we know not, reveal to us;
that which is wanting in us, fill in us;
that which we know, confirm in us,
and keep us blameless in Your service,
through the same Jesus Christ our Lord. Amen.

A PRAYER OF SAINT EPHREM THE SYRIAN

O Lord and Master of my life!
Take from me the spirit of sloth, faintheartedness,
lust of power, and idle talk.
But give rather the spirit of chastity, humility,
patience and love to Thy servant.

Yea, O Lord and King!
Grant me to see my own errors and not to judge
my brother; for Thou art blessed unto ages of ages. Amen.

A PRAYER BY SAINT PIO OF PIETRELCINA

May your heart be always the temple of the Holy Spirit.
May Jesus always be the helmsman of your spiritual ship.
May Mary be the star which shines on your path
and may she show you the safe way to
reach the Heavenly Father. Amen.

PSALM 8

O Lord, our Sovereign, how majestic is Your Name in all the earth!

You have set Your glory above the heavens.
Out of the mouths of babes and infants
You have founded a bulwark because of Your foes,
to silence the enemy and the avenger.

When I look at Your heavens, the work of Your fingers,
the moon and the stars that You have established;
what are human beings that You are mindful of them,
mortals that You care for them?

Yet You have made them a little lower than God,
and crowned them with glory and honor.
You have given them dominion over the
works of Your hands; You have put all things
under their feet, all sheep and oxen, and also
the beasts of the field, the birds of the air,
and the fish of the sea, whatever
passes along the paths of the seas.
O Lord, our Sovereign, how majestic is Your Name in all the earth!

AFFIRMATION OF SAINT CATHERINE OF SIENA

I trust in the Lord Jesus Christ; not in myself.

THE ASCENSION OF JESUS CHRIST
MARK 16:19; LUKE 24:50-52; ACTS 1: 6-12
"EVERY KNEE SHALL BOW, EVERY TONGUE CONFESS THAT JESUS CHRIST IS LORD"

On the fortieth day after the Resurrection, Jesus appeared to His disciples and gave them His last commandment - to preach the Kingdom of God and the repentance and forgiveness of sins in His name to all nations.

"Then he led them out as far as Bethany, and lifting up his hands he blessed them. While he blessed them, he parted from them, and was carried up into heaven." Luke 24:50-51

While the disciples were looking up at the sky, two angels in white robes appeared and said to them:

"Men of Galilee, why do you stand looking into heaven? This Jesus, who was taken up from you into heaven, will come in the same way as you saw him go into heaven." Acts 1:11

Jesus completed His earthly mission of bringing salvation to all people and was lifted up from this world into heaven. He returned to the Father in heaven Who sent Him into the world. In ascending to the Father, He raises earth to heaven with Him.

As the angels said, Christ will return to the earth in the same manner as He left it. When the risen Lord returns again in glory, God's will for mankind will be fulfilled.

"Peace I leave with you; my peace I give to you;
not as the world gives do I give to you. Let not your hearts be troubled, neither let them be afraid. You heard me say to you, 'I go away, and I will come to you.' If you loved me, you would have rejoiced because I go to the Father; for the Father is greater than I. John 14:27-28

Come, Lord Jesus, come!

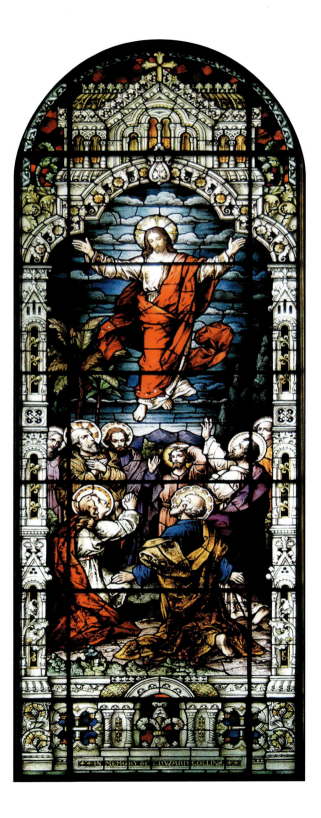

THE ASCENSION ICONOGRAPHY
Mark 16:19-20; Luke 24:50-53;
Acts 1:9-11

The Ascension narrative marks Christ's final appearance on earth until His Second Coming. Although the exact location is not clearly stated, the Gospel of Luke records that Christ took his apostles as far as Bethany, lifted up his hands and blessed them. While he was blessing them, "he parted from them, and was carried up into heaven" (Luke 24:51).

This majestic window depicts Christ with outstretched arms, triumphantly ascending upward into the clouds as He looks downward to the apostles below. His outstretched hands and His feet bear the wounds of His crucifion. Jesus is robed in red and white, symbolizing the sacrifice of love and purity offered up for us. His garment blows in the wind, but there is no clear up or down direction. This prefigures the Second Coming. Jesus is leaving, but He will return.

The apostles are symmetrically arranged along the lower zone of the window, looking upward with astonishment. Each figure has been carefully rendered and individualized. A variety of postures and gestures illustrates their amazement and wonder at the miraculous event unfolding before them. Although a positive identification of each apostle is debatable, two are recognizable and are significantly positioned among the remaining men: Saint Peter and Saint John. Saint Peter is the one to whom Jesus entrusts the leadership of the Church. Saint John the Beloved is the one to whom Jesus entrusted the care of His mother.

Saint Peter kneels in the lower right foreground. Like Saint Joseph, Saint Peter is typically painted in yellow dress. Here he wears a yellow mantle, the color symbolic of revealed truth, because it was he who declared, "You are the Christ, the Son of the living God" (Matthew 16:16). Saint Peter is generally distinguished by his short white hair and beard.

Saint John the Beloved wears a red mantle and white gown and is kneeling in the lower left foreground area, opposite to Peter. He is typically depicted as a beardless young man with fair hair. In groupings of the disciples, he is usually shown positioned near Christ. Both of these two men are emphasized in this scene by their prominent placement: kneeling, with backs turned to the viewer, their bodies form the base of an implied triangle that culminates with the ascending Christ above. Their strategic placement leads the viewer from the lower center of the window directly upward to Jesus, who enters into divine glory, symbolized by the clouds and the heavenly sky.

The visual source for the risen Christ in the upper half of the Ascension window is the revered painting *The Transfiguration* by the Italian master Raphael. Although left unfinished at the time of Raphael's death in 1520, the dynamic realism of *The Transfiguration* had a decisive impact on future generations of artists and was the most popular of all religious paintings adapted for stained glass in the first half of the nineteenth-century.

CHRIST THE KING

Lord Jesus Christ, You are the King of the whole world.
All that was made was created for You.
Exercise Your sovereign rights over me.

I renew my baptismal vows, renouncing Satan
with all his works and his false glamour, and
I promise to live as a good Christian.

I pledge to do all in my power to make the rights
of God and of Your Church triumph in the world.
I offer You whatever I do, however feeble, to obtain
that all human hearts may admit Your sacred
kingship, so that the kingdom of Your peace will
be established throughout the world. Amen.

Blessings and glory, wisdom and thanksgiving, honor,
power and might, be to our God, forever and ever. Amen.

PRAYER FOR THE SEVEN GIFTS OF THE HOLY SPIRIT

O Lord Jesus Christ, Who, before ascending into heaven,
did promise to send the Holy Ghost to finish
Your work in the souls of Your apostles and disciples,
deign to grant the same Holy Spirit to me that He may
perfect in my soul the work of Your grace and Your love.

Grant me the Spirit of Wisdom, that I may despise
the perishable things of this world and aspire
only after the things that are eternal;

the Spirit of Understanding, to enlighten
my mind with the light of Your divine truth;

the Spirit of Counsel, that I may ever choose
the surest way of pleasing God and gaining heaven;

the Spirit of Fortitude, that I may bear my cross
with You and that I may overcome with courage
all the obstacles that oppose my salvation;

the Spirit of Knowledge, that I may know God and
know myself and grow perfect in the sciences of the Saints;

the Spirit of Piety, that I may find the service
of God sweet and amiable;

the Spirit of Fear, that I may be filled with a loving
reverence towards God and may dread in any way
to displease Him.

Mark me, dear Lord, with the sign of Your true disciples
and animate me in all things with Your Spirit. Amen.

PRAYER OF SAINT THOMAS MORE

Give me the grace to long for Your holy sacraments, and
especially to rejoice in the presence of Your body, sweet
Saviour Christ, in the Holy Sacrament of the altar. Amen.

A PRAYER OF SAINT ANTIOCHUS

O Only-Begotten Word of the Father,
Jesus Christ, Who alone are perfect:
according to the greatness of Your mercy, do not
abandon me, Your servant, but ever rest in my heart.

O sweet Jesus, Good Shepherd of Your flock, deliver
me from the attacks of the Enemy.
Do not allow me to become the prey of Satan's
evil intent, even though I have within me
the seed of eternal damnation.

Instead, O Lord Jesus Christ, Adorable God,
Holy King, while I sleep, protect me by Your Holy Spirit,
through whom You sanctified Your Apostles.

Enlighten my mind by the light of the Holy Gospel,
my soul by the love of Your Cross,
my heart by the purity of Your teaching.
Protect my body by Your sacred passion, my senses
by Your humility, and awaken me in

due time for Your glorification.
For You, above all, are adorable, together with
Your eternal Father, and the Holy Spirit, now and
ever, and forever. Amen.

ATTENDE DOMINE (HEARKEN, O LORD)

R: Hearken, O Lord, and have mercy,
for we have sinned against Thee

Crying, we raise our eyes to Thee,
Sovereign King, Redeemer of all.
Listen, Christ, to the pleas of the supplicant sinners. R.

Thou art at the Right Hand of God the Father,
the Keystone, the Way of salvation and Gate of Heaven,
cleanse the stains of our sins. R.

O God, we beseech Thy majesty to hear our groans;
to forgive our sins. R.

We confess to Thee our consented sins; we declare
our hidden sins with contrite heart;
in Thy mercy, O Redeemer, forgive them. R.

Thou wert captured, being innocent;
brought about without resistance, condemned by
impious men with false witnesses.
O Christ, keep safe those whom Thou hast redeemed. R.

AN ASPIRATION OF SAINT THERESE OF LISIEUX

Let us go forward in peace, our eyes upon heaven,
the only one goal of our labors. Amen.

PRAYER TO LORD JESUS CHRIST, KING OF KINGS

Lord Jesus Christ, King of kings, You
have power over life and death.
You know what is secret and hidden, and neither

our thoughts nor our feelings are concealed from You.
Cure me of duplicity; I have done evil before You.
Now, my life declines from day to day and my sins increase.

O Lord, God of souls and bodies, You know the
extreme frailty of my soul and my flesh.
Grant me strength in my weakness, O Lord,
and sustain me in my misery.
Give me a grateful soul that I may never cease to
recall Your benefits, O Lord most bountiful.

Be not mindful of my many sins, but forgive
me all my misdeeds.
O Lord, disdain not my prayer - the prayer
of a wretched sinner;
sustain me with Your grace until the end,
that it may protect me as in the past.

It is Your grace which has taught me wisdom;
blessed are they who follow her ways,
for they shall receive the crown of glory.

In spite of my unworthiness, I praise You and I glorify You,
O Lord, for Your mercy to me is without limit.
You have been my help and my protection.
May the name of Your majesty be praised forever.
To You, our God, be glory. Amen.

A PRAYER OF SAINT EPHREM THE SYRIAN

Receive, O Lord, in heaven above our
prayers and supplications pure:
Give us a heart all full of love and steady courage to endure.
Thy holy name our mouths confess;
our tongues are harps to praise Thy grace.
Forgive our sins and wickedness, who in
this vigil seek Thy face.
Let not our song become a sigh, a wail of anguish and
despair; In loving-kindness, Lord most high,
receive tonight our evening prayer. Amen.

A MARIAN PRAYER OF SAINT ANTHONY OF PADUA

Mary, our Queen, Holy Mother of God,
we beg you to hear our prayer.

Make our hearts overflow with divine grace
and, resplendent with heavenly wisdom,
render them strong with your might and rich in virtue.

Pour down upon us the gift of mercy so that
we may obtain the pardon of our sins.

Help us to live in such a way as to merit
the glory and bliss of heaven.

May this be granted to us by your Son
Jesus, Who has exalted you above the angels,
has crowned you as Queen, and has seated you
with Him forever on His refulgent throne. Amen.

TO JESUS CHRIST OUR SOVEREIGN KING

To Jesus Christ our Sovereign King
who is the world's salvation.
All praise and homage do we bring
and thanks and adoration.

Thy reign extend O King benign,
to every land and nation;
for in Thy kingdom Lord divine
alone we find salvation.

To Thee and to Thy Church, great King
we pledge our heart's oblation;
until before Thy throne we sing
in endless jubilation.

Christ Jesus, Victor!
Christ Jesus, Ruler!
Christ Jesus, Lord and Redeemer!

THE SACRED HEART OF JESUS

"From the depth of my nothingness, I prostrate myself before Thee, O Most Sacred, Divine and Adorable Heart of Jesus, to pay Thee all the homage of love, praise and adoration in my power. Amen." Saint Margaret Mary Alacoque

Saint Margaret Mary (1647-1690), a Visitation nun, had a personal revelation involving a series of visions of Jesus as she prayed before the Blessed Sacrament. Jesus emphasized His love and His woundedness caused by man's indifference to His love and explained the devotion to His Sacred Heart as He wanted people to practice it, asking that He be honored in the symbol of His Heart made flesh.

The Church approved the Devotion to the Sacred Heart based upon the visions of Saint Margaret Mary and on its own merits. Jesus is the incarnation of God's infinite love and the perfect model of love of God and neighbor. The devotion is focused on Christ's Heart of Flesh and Christ's love for us.

The meaning of love was especially evident in Jesus' sufferings. "The prayer of the Church venerates and honors the *Heart of Jesus* just as it invokes his most holy name. It adores the incarnate Word and his Heart which, out of love for men, he allowed to be pierced by our sins" Catechism. P:2669. Out of love for His Father, He willed to undergo the death of the Cross. "My Father, if it is possible, let this cup pass from me; yet, not as I will, but as you will" (Matthew 26:39). The devotion focuses on the fact that He also walked that road to Calvary because of His love for us.

"No one has greater love than this, to lay down one's life for one's friends" John 15:13.

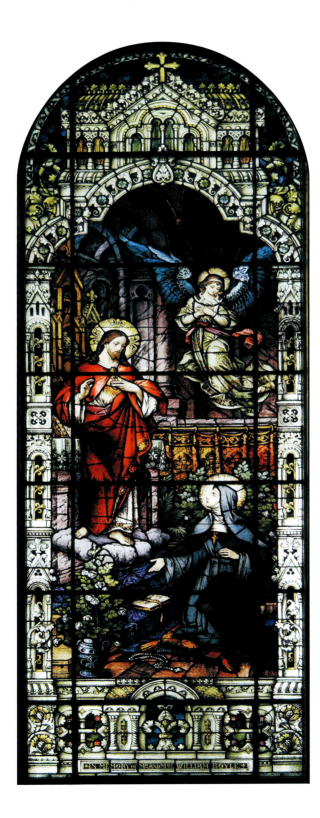

SAINT MARGARET MARY ALACOQUE AND
THE SACRED HEART OF JESUS ICONOGRAPHY

Saint Margaret Mary Alacoque (1647-1690) was a religious of the Visitation Order at the Convent of Paray-le-Monial in Burgundy. She entered the convent at the age of twenty-four and pronounced her final vows the following year. Between the years 1673 and 1675, Saint Margaret Mary, an ardent advocate of devotion to the Sacred Heart of Jesus, had many mystical revelations in which Jesus appeared to her. These visions were not the source of the devotion to the Sacred Heart of Jesus, but were significant in helping to spread the devotion and in shaping its practices.

The private revelations to Sister Margaret Mary have formed the basis for the iconography of the Sacred Heart in Christian art. The heart, the symbol of love, is popularly depicted with a wound, encircled by a crown of thorns and a small cross above, the whole radiating golden light. The Sacred Heart of Jesus in the window scene follows this traditional representation.

Saint Margaret Mary is shown dressed in the habit of her Order. She kneels on the altar steps with her arms flung open, her rosary having dropped onto the floor beside her when she was surprised during her devotions. Jesus stands before her, suspended on a white cloud before the lace-covered altar, His right hand raised in blessing and His left hand pointing to His Sacred Heart. Symbolic of the Trinity, Jesus' head is surrounded by an elaborate white and gold nimbus.

The open book lying on the altar step before Saint Margaret Mary symbolizes the wisdom brought by Christ. The vase of blue flowers symbolizes His spiritual love. The closeness of Christ's body to the altar and the golden ciborium within the open tabernacle encourages the viewer to reflect upon His Real Presence in the Eucharist, just as he is physically present before Saint Margaret Mary. A youthful angel, God's heavenly messenger and companion, hovers with beautiful blue wings above this divine apparition.

ACT OF CONSECRATION TO THE SACRED HEART BY SAINT MARGARET MARY ALACOQUE

O Sacred Heart of Jesus, to Thee I consecrate and offer up my person and my life, my actions, trials and sufferings, that my entire being may henceforth only be employed in loving, honoring and glorifying Thee. This is my irrevocable will, to belong entirely to Thee, and to do all for Thy love, renouncing with my whole heart all that can displease Thee.

I Take Thee, O Sacred Heart, for the sole object of my love, the protection of my life, the pledge of my salvation, the remedy of my frailty and inconstancy, the reparation for all the defects of my life, and my secure refuge at the hour of my death.

Be Thou, O Most Merciful Heart, my justification before God Thy Father, and screen me from His anger which I have so justly merited.
I fear all from my own weakness and malice, but placing my entire confidence in Thee, O Heart of Love, I hope all from Thine Infinite Goodness.

Annihilate in me all that can displease or resist Thee. Imprint Thy pure love so deeply in my heart that I may never forget Thee or be separated from Thee.

I beseech Thee, through Thine Infinite Goodness, grant that my name be engraved upon Thy Heart, for in this I place all my happiness and all my glory, to live and to die as one of Thy devoted servants. Amen.

PRAYER TO THE SACRED HEART

I fly to you Sacred Heart of my Saviour, for You are my refuge, my only hope. You are the remedy for all my misery, my consolation in all my wretchedness, the reparation for all my infidelity, the supplement for all my deficiency, the expiation for all my sins, and the hope and end of all my prayers.

You are the only one who is never weary of me
and who can bear with my faults, because You
love me with an infinite love.

Therefore, O my God, have mercy on me according to
Your great mercy, and do with me, and for me, whatever
You will, for I give myself entirely to You, Divine Heart,
with full confidence that You will never reject me. Amen.

A MORNING PRAYER WRITTEN BY SAINT THERESE OF LISIEUX

O my God! I offer Thee all my actions of this day for the
intentions and for the glory of the Sacred Heart of Jesus.
I desire to sanctify every beat of my heart, my every
thought, my simplest works, by uniting them to Its
Infinite Merits; and I wish to make reparation for my sins
by casting them into the furnace of Its Merciful Love.

O my God! I ask of Thee for myself and for those whom I
hold dear, the grace to fulfill perfectly Thy Holy Will,
to accept for love of Thee the joys and sorrows of
this passing life, so that we may one day be united
together in heaven for all eternity. Amen.

PRAYER TO THE SACRED HEART OF JESUS BY SAINT GERTRUDE

O Sacred Heart of Jesus, fountain of eternal life,
Your Heart is a glowing furnace of love.
You are my refuge and my sanctuary.
O My adorable and loving Saviour, consume my heart
with the burning fire with which Yours is aflame.
Pour down on my soul those graces
which flow from Your love.
Let my heart be united with Yours.
Let my will be conformed to Yours in all things.
May Your Will be the rule of all my desires and actions. Amen.

PRAYER FOR CHRIST'S MERCY BY SAINT JEROME

O Lord, show Your mercy to me and gladden my heart.
I am like the man on the way to Jericho who was

overtaken by robbers, wounded and left for dead.
O Good Samaritan, come to my aid.

I am like the sheep that went astray.
O Good Shepherd, seek me out and bring me
home in accord with Your will.

Let me dwell in Your house all the days of my life
and praise You for ever and ever with those
who are there. Amen.

JESUS, THOU JOY OF LOVING HEARTS BY SAINT BERNARD OF CLAIRVAUX

Jesus, Thou joy of loving hearts, Thou fount of life, Thou
light of men; from the poor bliss that earth imparts,
we turn unfilled to Thee again.

Thy truth unchanged hath ever stood; Thou savest
those who on Thee call; to them that seek Thee,
Thou art good; to them that find Thee, all in all.

We taste Thee, O Thou living bread, and long to feast
upon Thee still; we drink of Thee the fountain-head,
and thirst our souls from Thee to fill.

Our restless spirits yearn for Thee, where'er our changeful
lot is cast; glad, when Thy gracious smile we see;
blest, when our faith can hold Thee fast.

O Jesus, ever with us stay; make all our moments calm
and bright; chase the dark night of sin away; shed
o'er the world Thy holy light. Amen.

REFLECTION OF SAINT TERESA OF AVILA

We shall never learn to know ourselves except by endeavoring
to know God: for beholding His greatness, we realize
our own littleness; His purity shows us our foulness;
and by meditating upon His humility, we find how
very far we are from being humble.

PRAYER OF SAINT THERESE LISIEUX

My Lord and my God, I have realized that whoever
undertakes to do anything for the sake of earthly things
or to earn the praise of others deceives himself.
Today one thing pleases the world; tomorrow another.
What is praised on one occasion is denounced on another.
Blessed be You, my Lord and my God,
for You are unchangeable for all eternity.
Whoever serves You faithfully to the end will enjoy
life without end in eternity. Amen.

PRAYER TO THE SACRED HEART OF JESUS BY SAINT PIO OF PIETRELCINA

O Sacred Heart of Jesus, filled with infinite love, broken by my
ingratitude, pierced by my sins, yet loving me still; accept the
consecration that I make to You of all that I am and all that I have.
Take every faculty of my soul and body and draw me, day by day,
nearer and nearer to Your Sacred Heart, and there, as I can
understand the lesson, teach me Your blessed ways. Amen.

THE GOLDEN ARROW PRAYER

May the most holy, most sacred, most adorable,
most incomprehensible and ineffable
Name of God be forever praised, blessed, loved,
adored and glorified in Heaven, on earth, and
under the earth, by all the creatures of God,
and by the Sacred Heart of Our Lord Jesus Christ,
in the Most Holy Sacrament of the altar. Amen.

PSALM 134

Come, bless the Lord, all you servants of the Lord,
who stand by night in the house of the Lord!
Lift up your hands to the holy place,
and bless the Lord.

May the Lord, maker of heaven and earth,
bless you from Zion.

THE FINDING IN THE TEMPLE
LUKE 2: 41-52
"DID YOU NOT KNOW
THAT I MUST BE IN MY FATHER'S HOUSE?"

The feast of Passover occurs at the time of the full moon during the month of Nisan, which begins in March and ends in April. In ancient Israel each Jewish family was encouraged to travel to Jerusalem to the Temple for this feast. Joseph and Mary traveled from Nazareth every year. When Jesus was twelve, He was "lost" in the Temple.

"Now his parents went to Jerusalem every year at the feast of Passover. And when he was twelve years old, they went up according to custom; and when the feast was ended, as they were returning, the boy Jesus stayed behind in Jerusalem. His parents did not know it, but supposing him to be in the company they went a day's journey, and they sought him among their kinsfolk and acquaintances; and when they did not find him, they returned to Jerusalem, seeking him. After three days they found him in the temple, sitting among the teachers, listening to them and asking them questions; and all who heard him were amazed at his understanding and his answers. And when they saw him they were astonished; and his mother said to him, 'Son, why have you treated us so? Behold, your father and I have been looking for you anxiously.'

Jesus was surprised they did not know exactly where to find him. Where else should they look for Him but in the Temple?

"How is it that you sought me? Did you not know that I must be in my Father's house?"

Jesus is there waiting for us in the tabernacle.
He is always in His Father's House.
We find Him truly present there.

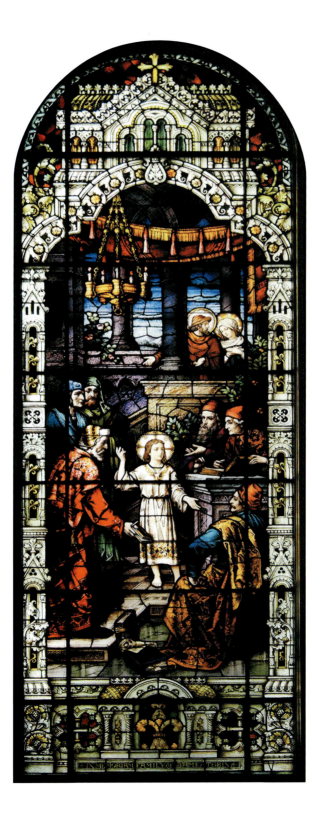

IN MEMORIAM FAMILY OF [...]

THE FINDING OF THE CHILD JESUS IN THE TEMPLE ICONOGRAPHY
Luke 2:41-52

The only incident from the childhood of Christ recorded in the Gospels tells the story of the loss of the Child and His subsequent discovery in the Temple. The twelve-year-old Jesus had accompanied his parents on their annual pilgrimage to Jerusalem for the Feast of the Passover. When the celebration ended, Mary and Joseph began the journey home, but after traveling on for a day, they discovered that He was missing and returned to Jerusalem to search for Him. The window illustrates the moment when they find the Boy in the Temple, listening to and asking questions of the elders and scribes. At the tender age of twelve, Jesus already showed signs of possessing great wisdom, for "all that heard him were astonished at his understanding and his answers" (Luke 2:47).

Wearing elaborate headdresses and richly patterned garments, the elders and scribes gesture and look toward Jesus as they engage in a captivating discourse with the young Boy. A variety of books and scrolls are available to assist the elders and also serve to signify the great wisdom and knowledge they possess. The elders direct their attention to the young, barefoot Jesus who, in contrast, stands alone in their midst, confidently and freely expounding on the sacred writings, thus demonstrating His unique relationship to God the Father.

Jesus is dressed in a sinple white and gold tunic that visually separates Him from the elders in their brightly colored garments. A variety of books and scrolls assist the elders and symbolize the wisdom and knowledge they possess. The scroll and books also signify that Jesus came to fulfill both the law and the prophets (Matthew 5:17).

Standing in the loggia at the top of the stairs are Saint Joseph and the Blessed Virgin. Mary wears a blue robe and a white veil, looking down on the scene. She stands with clasped hands veil, looking down on the scene. She stands with clasped hands across her chest. Her presence is symbolized by the lemon bush and the wild pink rose, both of which are aligned near her. The lemon is a symbol of fidelity and appears often with Mary. The rose is a frequent Marian symbol as well. The five petals of the wild rose are equated with the five joys of Mary as well as the five letters in her name, Maria. This numerical symbolism is continued also in the five candles located in the hanging lamp, although they may be interpreted as alluding to the five wounds of Christ. Mary wears the distinctive star nimbus (Revelation 12:1).

Saint Joseph stands next to his spouse, looking toward her and gesturing with both hands at the grouping below. He wears his hat and customary yellow-orange robe.

The scene represented in the window occurs before Mary and Joseph question His presence in the Temple. Jesus replies: "Why were you searching for me? Did you not know that I must be in my Father's house?" (Luke 2:49).

PRAYER OF SAINT BENEDICT FOR THE GIFTS TO SEEK GOD

Father, in Your goodness grant me the intellect
to comprehend You, the perception to discern You,
and the reason to appreciate You.

In Your kindness endow me with the diligence
to look for You, the wisdom to discover You,
and the spirit to apprehend You.

In Your graciousness bestow on me
a heart to contemplate You,
ears to hear You, eyes to see You,
and a tongue to speak of You.

In Your mercy confer on me a conversation
pleasing to You, the patience to wait for You,
and the perseverance to long for You.

Grant me a perfect end - Your holy presence. Amen.

FROM SAINT JEANNE JUGAN

Go and find Him when your patience and
strength run out and you feel alone and helpless.
Jesus is waiting for you in the chapel.
Say to Him, 'Jesus, You know exactly what is
going on. You are all I have, and You know
all things. Come to my help.'

And then go, and don't worry
about how you are going to manage.
That you have told God about it is enough.
He has a good memory.

PRAYER TO PRACTICE WHAT JESUS TAUGHT BY
SAINT APOLLONIUS OF ROME, MARTYR

O Lord Jesus Christ, grant us a measure of Your Spirit.
Help us to obey Your teaching, soothe anger, cultivate pity,
overcome desire, increase love, cast off sorrow, shun

vainglory, renounce revenge, and not be afraid of death.
Let us entrust our spirit to the everlasting God who with
You and the Holy Spirit lives and rules forever and ever. Amen.

A PRAYER OF ALFRED THE GREAT

We pray to You, O Lord, who are the
supreme Truth, and all truth is from You.

We beseech You, O Lord, who are the highest Wisdom,
and all wise depend on You for their wisdom.
You are the supreme Joy, and all
who are happy owe it to You.

You are the Light of minds, and all receive their
understanding from You.

We love, we love You above all.
We seek You, we follow You, and we are
ready to serve You.

We desire to dwell under Your power
for You are the King of all. Amen.

A PRAYER OF SAINT COLUMBA

Be, Lord Jesus, a bright flame before me,
a guiding star above me, a smooth path below me,
a kindly shepherd behind me:
today, tonight, and forever. Amen

A PRAYER OF SAINT THOMAS MORE

O Lord, give us a mind that is humble, quiet,
peaceable, patient, and charitable.
And a taste of Your Holy Spirit in all our thoughts,
words, and deeds.
O Lord, give us a lively faith, a firm hope,
a fervent charity, a love of You.
Take from us all lukewarmness in meditation
and dullness in prayer.

Give us fervor and delight in thinking of You,
Your grace, and Your tender compassion toward us.
Give us, good Lord, the grace to work
for the things we pray for. Amen.

A PRAYER OF JOHN HENRY CARDINAL NEWMAN

I need Thee to teach me day by day, according
to each day's opportunities and needs.

Give me, O my Lord, that purity of conscience which
alone can receive Thy inspirations.
My ears are dull, so I cannot hear Thy voice.
My eyes are dim, so that I cannot see Thy tokens.
Thou alone canst quicken my hearing, and purge my
sight, and cleanse and renew my heart.
Teach me to sit at Thy feet, and to hear Thy word. Amen.

A PRAYER OF SAINT ANSELM

O Lord my God, teach my heart this
day where and how to find You.
You have made me and re-made me, and
You have bestowed on me all the good things I
possess, and still I do not know You.
I have not yet done that for which I was made.

Teach me to seek You, for I cannot seek You
unless You teach me, or find You unless
You show Yourself to me.

Let me seek You in my desire; let me desire
You in my seeking. Let me find You by loving
You; let me love You when I find You. Amen

A PRAYER OF
SAINT EDITH STEIN (TERESA BENEDICTA OF THE CROSS)

O Lord God, will to give me all that leads to You.
O Lord God, take away from me
all that diverts me from You.

O Lord God, take me also, from myself
and give me completely to Yourself. Amen.

A PRAYER BY POPE CLEMENT XI

I pray, Lord, that You enlighten my mind, inflame my will,
purify my heart, and sanctify my soul. Amen.

A PRAYER OF SAINT BONAVENTURE

Lord Jesus, as God's Spirit came down and rested upon You,
may the same Spirit rest on us, bestowing His sevenfold gifts.
First, grant us the gift of understanding,
by which Your precepts may enlighten our minds.
Second, grant us counsel, by which we may follow in
Your footsteps on the path of righteousness.
Third, grant us courage, by which we may
ward off the enemy's attacks.
Fourth, grant us knowledge, by which we can
distinguish good from evil.
Fifth, grant us piety, by which we may draw back
from evil and submit to what is good.
Seventh, grant us wisdom, that we may taste fully the
life-giving sweetness of Your love. Amen.

PRAYER OF SAINT AUGUSTINE OF HIPPO
TO THE HOLY SPIRIT

Breathe into me, Spirit of God, that I may think what is holy.
Drive me, Spirit of God, that I may do what is holy.
Draw me, Spirit of God, that I may love what is holy.
Strengthen me, Spirit of God, that I may preserve what is holy.
Guide me, Spirit of God, that I may never lose what is holy. Amen.

A PRAYER OF SAINT THOMAS AQUINAS

Grant me, O Lord my God, a mind to know You,
a heart to seek You, wisdom to find You,
conduct pleasing to You,
faithful perseverance in waiting for You,
a hope of finally embracing You. Amen.

A PRAYER BEFORE CONFESSION BY SAINT GERTRUDE

O God, Father of light, who enlightens
everyone that comes into this world:
give me light, love and sorrow that I may
discover, detest and confess
all the sins I have committed.

O Holy Spirit of love and dispenser of all graces,
help me to receive this great sacrament worthily,
give me Thy grace that I may make a careful
examination of conscience and discover my sins.

Touch my heart that I may hate and detest
them and assist me to make a firm resolution
to avoid sin henceforth.

Spirit of love and truth, assist me to make
a sincere, entire, and truthful confession
to Thy representative, the priest,
and thus obtain Thy forgiveness, Thy grace,
and Thy love, O Jesus my Redeemer,
through Thy most holy merits.

Grant me the grace to make this
confession well that I may glorify Thee.

O most holy Virgin Mary, Mother of my Saviour,
and my own most loving Mother, thou who are
so compassionate towards those who
desire to repent, help me to call to mind
all my offenses and to be truly sorry
for having offended God.

My dear Guardian Angel, who has been
a witness of my sins, help me now to recall
them and to be truly sorry for them.

All you saints and angels of heaven,
pray for me that I may now bring forth
fruits worthy of penance. Amen.

JESUS GIVES SAINT PETER THE KEYS OF THE KINGDOM
MATTHEW 16: 18-19
"FEED MY SHEEP"

Jesus chose twelve men to be with Him and to participate in His mission. Simon Peter was given a unique mission by Jesus. As the Catechism of the Catholic Church says, "Through a revelation from the Father, Peter had confessed: 'You are the Christ, the Son of the living God.' Our Lord then declared to him: 'You are Peter, and on this rock I will build my Church, and the gates of Hades will not prevail against it.'" (552)

In the Gospel of Matthew, Jesus went on to bestow special power upon Peter:

I will give you the keys of the kingdom of heaven, and
whatever you bind on earth shall be bound in heaven,
and whatever you loose on earth shall be loosed in heaven.

The power of the keys denotes Peter's special authority to govern the house of God. "The power to 'bind and loose' connotes the authority to absolve sins, to pronounce doctrinal judgments, and to make disciplinary decisions in the Church. Jesus entrusted this authority to the Church through the ministry of the apostles and in particular through the ministry of Peter, the only one to whom he specifically entrusted the keys of the kingdom." (553)

After Jesus' resurrection, He again singled out Peter, asking him three times, "Simon, son of John, do you love me more than these?" John 21:15,16,17. Each time Peter responded, "Yes, Lord." Jesus commissioned Peter to feed His lambs, tend His sheep, and feed His sheep.

"Ubi Petrus, ibi ecclesia
(Where Peter is, there is the Church)!"

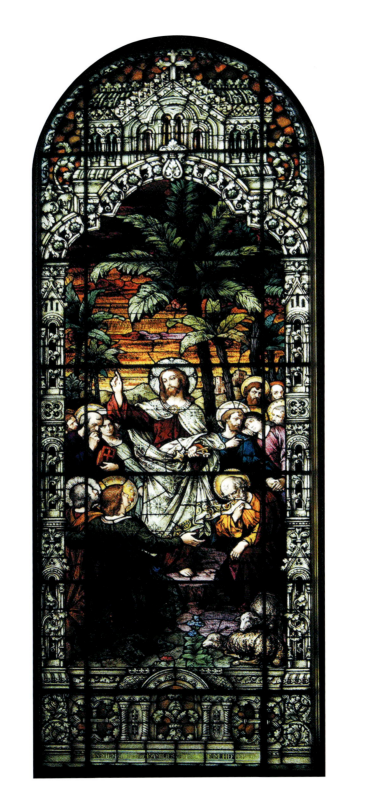

THE PRESENTATION OF THE KEYS OF THE KINGDOM
ICONOGRAPHY
Matthew 16:13-20; John 21:15-17

While Jesus and His apostles were traveling in the region of Caesarea Philippi, He asked them: "Who do men say that the Son of man is?" (Matthew 16: 13). Peter, the first apostle to make this confession, replied: "You are the Christ, the Son of the living God" (Matthew 16:16). The Primacy of Peter is based upon Jesus' commission to him: "I will give you the keys of the kingdom of heaven, and whatever you bind on earth shall be bound in heaven, and whatever you loose on earth shall be loosed in heaven" (Matthew 16:19).

Placed within a natural landscape, Jesus is elevated on a stone dais and stands in the midst of His apostles. He wears a red robe covered by an elaborately embroidered white mantle bearing the fleur-de-lis and is similar to the attire He wears in other narratives. Jesus' right hand is raised in a gesture of authority and public address, while His left firmly grasps two keys directly above Peter's head. Peter humbly kneels at the feet of Jesus while reverently kissing the mantle hem of his Master. In choosing to follow Jesus, Peter too is destined for a martyr's death.

The two crossed keys are Saint Peter's special attribute, and symbolize the authority entrusted to him, the first Pope, and to all of his successors. They are the principal insignia of the papacy and figure on the coat of arms of Vatican City. One is silver and the other gold, symbolizing his dual powers to bind or loose. In the window primroses are centered in the lower foreground and directly under the keys. Primroses are also called "keys of Heaven," or "St. Peter's keys."

Two sheep share the right foreground space of the composition and are nestled close to the primroses and Saint Peter. The inclusion of the animals directly refers to Christ's giving Peter the jurisdiction of supreme shepherd and ruler over the flock of the

Church. His repeated charge to Peter to "Feed my lambs," and "Feed my sheep," (John 21:15-17) further substantiates the unique mission given to Peter. The combined iconography of the keys and the sheep is symbolic of the pastoral office held by Peter that belongs to the Church's very foundation and is continued by the bishops under the primacy of the Pope, Peter's successor.

DIOCESE OF SAVANNAH PRAYER FOR VOCATIONS

O my God, hear my prayer and let my cry come unto You.
Bless our Diocese of Savannah with many
priestly and religious vocations.
Give the men and women You call the light to
understand Your gift and the love to follow
always in the footsteps of Your priestly Son. Amen.

PRAYER, YEAR FOR PRIESTS,
JUNE 19, 2009 - JUNE 19, 2010

Dear Lord, We pray that the Blessed Mother
wrap her mantle around Your priests
and through her intercession
strengthen them for their ministry.

We pray that Mary will guide Your priests
to follow her own words,
"Do whatever He tells you" (Jn.2:5).

May Your priests have the heart of St. Joseph,
Mary's most chaste spouse.

May the Blessed Mother's own pierced heart
inspire them to embrace
all who suffer at the foot of the cross.

May Your priests be holy,
filled with the fire of Your love,
seeking nothing but Your greater glory
and the salvation of souls. Amen.

Saint John Vianney, pray for us.

A PRAYER FOR THE POPE

Lord, source of eternal life and truth, give to Your
shepherd, the Pope, a spirit of courage and
right judgment, a spirit of knowledge and love.

By governing with fidelity those entrusted to
his care may he, as successor to the apostle
Peter and vicar of Christ, build Your church
into a sacrament of unity, love, and
peace for all the world.

We ask this through our Lord Jesus Christ, Your Son,

SAINT THERESE OF LISIEUX'S PRAYER FOR PRIESTS

O Jesus, eternal Priest, keep Your priests
within the shelter of Your Sacred Heart,
where none may touch them.

Keep unstained their anointed hands,
which daily touch Your Sacred Body.
Keep unsullied their lips, daily purpled
with Your Precious Blood.

Keep pure and earthly their hearts, sealed with
the sublime mark of the priesthood.

Let Your holy love surround them and shield
them from the world's contagion.

Bless their labors with abundant fruit and may the
souls to whom they minister be their joy and
consolation here and in heaven their beautiful
and everlasting crown. Amen

SAINT JOHN CHRYSOSTOM

He who honors a priest honors Christ;
he who insults a priest insults Christ.

SAINT FRANCIS OF ASSISI'S VOCATION PRAYER

Most High, Glorious God, enlighten
the darkness of our minds.
Give us a right faith, a firm hope and a

perfect charity, so that we may always and in
all things act according to Your Holy Will. Amen.

" MARIAN PRAYER FOR PRIESTS" OF SAINT CHARLES BORROMEO

O Holy Mother of God, pray for the priests
your Son has chosen to serve the church.

Help them by your intercession,
to be holy, zealous and chaste.
Make them models of virtue in the
service of God's people.

Help them to be prayerful in meditations,
effective in preaching, and enthusiastic
in the daily offering of the holy
sacrifice of the Mass.

Help them to administer the
sacraments with joy. Amen.

A HOLY HOUR FOR PRIESTS

My God, poor, weak and miserable as I am,
I have come to spend this hour alone with You,
in reparation for the priests who have forgotten
that they are Your chosen souls.

Especially, dear God, do I offer this holy hour
for the priests who at this moment need it most.
In praying for consecrated souls,
help me to remember my own utter weakness,
misery and nothingness.
Were it not for Your grace, I would be far
worse than those for whom I pray.

O My God, help those priests who are
faithful to remain faithful.
To those who are falling, stretch forth
Your Divine Hand that they may
grasp it as their support.

And for those poor unfortunate souls
who have fallen, lift them up in the great
ocean of Your Mercy, that being engulfed
therein, they may receive the grace to return
to Your Great Loving Heart. Amen.

APOSTOLIC PRAYER OF SAINT VINCENT PALLOTTI

Eternal Father, it is Your will
that all should be saved. Great is Your mercy.
Your Son, Jesus Christ, died for all.
Teach all people to recognize You and love You.
With deep faith in Christ's death
and resurrection, we pray:
Send forth, O Lord, laborers into Your vineyard
and spare Your people.
Eternal Word, Redeemer of all creation,
convert all souls to You.
You have been obedient for all,
even to death on the cross.

Look upon the merits of Your Mother
and of all the angels and saints
who intercede for us.
Send forth, O Lord, laborers into
Your vineyard and spare Your people.

O Holy Spirit, through the infinite merits of
our Lord, Jesus Christ, enkindle in all hearts
Your ardent love that can do all things, that
all may be one fold and one shepherd,
and that all may arrive in heaven
to sing Your Divine Mercy.

Queen of Apostles and all the angels and saints,
pray to the Lord of the harvest:
Send forth, O Lord, laborers into Your vineyard
and spare Your people, that united with You,
and the Father and the Holy Spirit,
we may all rejoice forever. Amen.

Who lives and reigns with You and the Holy Spirit,
one God, forever and ever. Amen.

PRAYER TO OUR LADY OF GUADALUPE

Our Lady of Guadalupe, mystical Rose,
intercede for the Church, protect the Holy Father,
help all who invoke you in their necessities.

Since you are the ever Virgin Mary
and Mother of the true God,
obtain for us from your most Holy Son,
the grace of a firm faith and sure hope
amid the bitterness of life, as well as
an ardent love and the precious gift
of final perseverance. Amen

A PRAYER FOR THE HOLY CHURCH AND FOR PRIESTS
BY SAINT MARIA FAUSTINA KOWALSKA

O my Jesus, I beg You on behalf of the whole Church:
grant it love and the light of Your Spirit
and give power to the words of priests
so that hardened hearts might be brought
to repentance and return to You, O Lord.

Lord, give us holy priests;
You Yourself maintain them in holiness.
O Divine and Great High Priest,
may the power of Your mercy accompany
them everywhere and protect them
from the devil's traps and snares which
are continually being set for the souls of priests.
May the power of Your mercy, O Lord,
shatter and bring to naught all
that might tarnish the sanctity of priests,
for You can do all things.

I ask You, Jesus, for a special blessing and for
light for the priests before whom I will make my
confessions throughout my lifetime. Amen.

THE DEATH OF SAINT JOSEPH
"JOSEPH HER HUSBAND WAS A RIGHTEOUS MAN"

Joseph, a descendant of the great King David, was an observant Jew. He obeyed God's instructions when Jesus was eight days' old (Luke 2:21). Forty days after Jesus' birth, Joseph took Mary and the baby Jesus to the Temple in Jerusalem to fulfill the requirements of God's law (Luke 2:22-24). Every year, Joseph would travel to the Temple with Mary to celebrate the Passover.

Joseph says nothing in the Gospels, but his actions speak volumes. He was a righteous man, who had compassion on Mary when he believed she had betrayed him with another man (Matthew 1:19). God's angel appeared to Joseph, revealing that the apparent tragedy was God's work. Joseph immediately took the pregnant Mary into his home.

He provided for Mary and Jesus: travel to Bethlehem, shelter for the birth and later safety in Egypt from the murderous Herod. Repeatedly, Joseph obeyed God's angel. Satan himself was defeated by this simple man's obedience to the will of God.

When the threat to the child Jesus' life was past, Joseph took his family home to Nazareth. Again, he obeyed the will of God. Joseph was patient. He waited for God's orders before acting.

Joseph last appears in the scriptures when Jesus was twelve. After a trip to the temple in Jerusalem, Joseph and Mary were separated from the child. Frantically, they search for the boy for three days, only to find Him safe in the Temple, speaking with the scribes and elders. Christ returned to Nazareth and was obedient to Joseph and Mary (Luke 2:51).

Joseph's unquestioning faithfulness to the will of God obtained for him, in the words of Saint Alphonsus Ligouri, " special power against the evil spirits, who tempt us with redoubled vigor at the hour of death."

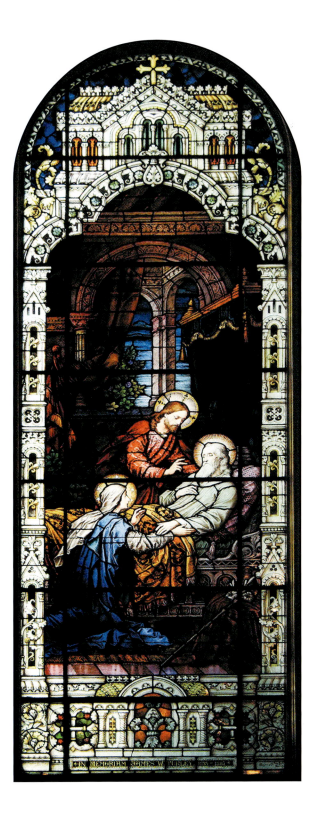

THE DEATH OF SAINT JOSEPH ICONOGRAPHY

Public recognition of Saint Joseph is first found among the Eastern Copts in the fourth century. A Coptic manuscript, The *History of Joseph the Carpenter*, dates to this period. The manuscript describes St. Joseph's death as occurring in the presence of both Jesus and Mary. This window scene offers a faithful rendering of that narrative.

Joseph lies on his deathbed while Jesus leans forward to offer a blessing. Mary kneels on the opposite side of the bed, demonstrating her devotion as her arms reach outward to comfort her dying husband. The opulent interior decorations and furniture provide a colorful background for the pale and seemingly fragile figure of Joseph. His attribute, the white lily, is symbolic of his chastity and is noticeably visible. Lilies appear again In the decorative relief design along the side of the bed, within the carved arcade of round arches.

Another of Joseph's attributes is the lily-topped rod, visible in the lower right area of the window, propped against a stool placed near his bed. The origin of this attribute is the *The Golden Legend*, a popular medieval book of saints' lives, written about 1260 by Jacobus de Voragine. According to *The Golden Legend*, eligible suitors for Mary were to present rods to the high priest. Mary's hand would be granted to the one whose rod bloomed. Joseph brought his branch forward, and it immediately flowered.

After the Council of Trent (1545-1563), Saint Joseph was honored as patron of the dying or of a holy death. Although generated in the East from the sixth century, the cult of Joseph was greatly extended in the West during the Counter-Reformation by the Jesuits and especially in Spain by Saint Theresa of Avila.

Jospeh was regarded as a faithful companion to lead the dying through the last rite of passage. Images of the Saint's death became a popular subject and a source of comfort for the dying. During the late nineteenth and early twentieth centuries, the image of St. Joseph dying, accompanied by Jesus and Mary, was a popular subject for stained glass windows as well as colored lithographs produced for family and domestic devotions. The Franz Mayer window scene is closely modeled after the painting, *The Death of Joseph*, c. 1712 by the Italian late Baroque painter, Giuseppe Maria Crespi ("Lo Soagnolo").

The source of Joseph's rapid rise in popularity during the last half of the nineteenth century is directly attributed to major papal pronouncements honoring the Saint. In 1847, Pope Pius IX extended to the Universal Church the feast of the Patronage of Saint Joseph. In 1870 the *Quemadmodum Deus* proclaimed Saint Joseph to be the Patron of the Universal Church. Pope Leo XIII issuing *Quamquam Pluries* in 1889, stressed the importance of the patronage of Saint Joseph and the continuance of special devotion to him. Additionally, a significant body of religious literature of the period attests to the prevalence of invoking Saint Joseph as protector at the hour of death, the basis of which is set forth in a mid-nineteenth century devotional manual, *The Devout Client of St. Joseph*

A PRAYER OF SAINT MACARIUS OF EGYPT

Lord, be merciful now that my life is approaching
its end, and the evening awaits me.
There is not enough time for me to cleanse myself
of my sins, for they are so many.
Heal me while I am still on earth, and I shall be truly healthy.
In Your mercy, move me to repent so that
I shall not be ashamed when I meet You in heaven. Amen.

ANCIENT PRAYER TO SAINT JOSEPH

O St. Joseph, whose protection is so great, so strong,
so prompt before the throne of God,
I place in thee all my interests and desires.
O St. Joseph, assist me by thy powerful intercession
and obtain for me all spiritual blessing through thy foster Son,
Jesus Christ Our Lord, so that, having engaged here below thy
heavenly power, I may offer thee my thanksgiving and homage.

O St. Joseph, I never weary contemplating
thee and Jesus asleep in thine arms.
I dare not approach while He reposes near thy heart.
Press Him in my name and kiss His fine head for me, and
ask Him to return the kiss when I draw my dying breath.

St. Joseph, Patron of departing souls, pray for me. Amen.

A PRAYER BY THE BLESSED MOTHER TERESA OF CALCUTTA

Heavenly Father, You have given us a model
of life in the Holy Family of Nazareth.
Help us, O loving Father to make our family another
Nazareth where love, peace and joy reign.
May it be deeply contemplative, intensely
Eucharistic and vibrant with joy.
Help us to stay together in joy and sorrow
through family prayer.
Teach us to see Jesus in the members of our family,
especially in their distressing disguise.
May the Eucharistic Heart of Jesus make our hearts

meek and humble like His and help us to
carry out our family duties in a holy way.
May we love one another as God loves each one of us
more and more each day, and forgive each
other's faults as You forgive our sins.
Help us, O loving Father to take whatever You give
and to give whatever You take with a big smile.

Immaculate Heart of Mary, cause of our joy, pray for us.
Saint Joseph, pray for us.
Holy Guardian Angels be always with us, guide
and protect us. Amen.

A PRAYER FOR THE SOULS IN PURGATORY

O gentle Heart of Jesus, ever present in the Blessed
Sacrament, ever consumed with burning love for the poor
captive souls in Purgatory, have mercy on them.
Be not severe in Your judgments, but let some drops of Your
precious Blood fall upon the devouring flames.
And merciful Saviour, send Your angels to conduct them to
a place of refreshment, light and peace. Amen.

A PRAYER FOR THE FAITHFUL DEPARTED

May the souls of the faithful departed, through the
mercy of God, rest in peace. Amen.

PRAYER FOR GOD'S SUPPORT BY JOHN HENRY CARDINAL NEWMAN

May He support us all the day long, till the shadows
lengthen, and the evening comes, and the busy world is
hushed, and the fever of life is over, and our work is done.
Then in His mercy, may He give us a safe
lodging, and a holy rest, and peace at last.

PRAYER FOR THE GRACE TO AGE WELL

When the signs of age begin to mark my body
(and still more when they touch my mind)

When the illness that is to diminish me or carry me off
strikes from without or is borne within me;
When the painful moment comes in which I awaken
to the fact that I am growing ill or growing old;
And above all at that last moment
When I feel I am losing hold of myself
and am absolutely passive within the hands
of the great unknown forces that have formed me;
In all these dark moments, O God,
grant that I may understand that it is You
(providing only my faith is strong enough)
Who is painfully parting the fibers of my being
in order to penetrate to the very marrow
of my substance and bear me away within Yourself.

PRAYER OF POPE JOHN XXIII TO SAINT JOSEPH FOR FATHERS

Saint Joseph, guardian of Jesus and chaste
husband of Mary, you passed your life in
loving fulfillment of duty.
You supported the holy family of Nazareth
with the work of your hands.
Kindly protect those who trustingly come to you.
You know their aspirations, their hardships, their hopes.
They look to you because they know you will
understand and protect them.
You too knew trial, labor and weariness.
But amid the worries of material life, your soul was full
of deep peace and sang out in true joy through
intimacy with God's Son entrusted to you
and with Mary, His tender Mother.
Assure those you protect that they do not labor alone.
Teach them to find Jesus near them and to watch over
Him faithfully as you have done. Amen.

FATIMA MORNING OFFERING

O Jesus, through the Immaculate Heart of Mary, I offer You my
prayers, works, joys, and suffering, all that this day may bring, be
they good or bad: for the love of God, for the conversion of

sinners, and in reparation for all the sins committed against the Sacred Heart and the Immaculate Heart of Mary. Amen.

"STAY WITH ME, LORD" BY SAINT PIO OF PIETRELCINA

Stay with me, Lord, for it is necessary to have
You present so that I do not forget You.
You know how easily I abandon You.
Stay with me, Lord, because I am weak and I need Your
strength, that I may not fall so often.
Stay with me, Lord, for You are my life, and
without You, I am without fervor.
Stay with me, Lord, for You are my light, and
without You, I am in darkness.
Stay with me, Lord, to show me Your will.
Stay with me, Lord, so that I hear Your voice and follow You.
Stay with me, Lord, for I desire to love You
very much, and always be in Your company.
Stay with me, Lord, if You wish me to be faithful to You.
Stay with me, Lord, for as poor as my soul is,
I want it to be a place of consolation for You, a nest of love.
Stay with me, Jesus, for it is getting late and the
day is coming to a close, and life passes;
death, judgment, eternity approaches.
It is necessary to renew my strength, so that I will not
stop along the way and for that, I need You.
It is getting late and death approaches.
I fear the darkness, the temptations, the dryness,
the cross, the sorrows.
O how I need You, my Jesus, in this night of exile!
Stay with me tonight, Jesus.
In life with all its dangers, I need You.
Let me recognize You as Your disciples did at the
breaking of the bread, so that the Eucharistic Communion
be the Light which disperses the darkness, the force
which sustains me, the unique joy of my heart.
Stay with me, Lord, because at the hour of my
death, I want to remain united to You, if not by
communion, at least by grace and love.
Stay with me, Jesus.
I do not ask for divine consolation, because

I do not merit it, but the gift of
Your Presence, oh, yes, I ask this of You!
Stay with me, Lord, for it is You alone I look for,
Your Love, Your Grace, Your Will, Your Heart,
Your Spirit, because I love You and ask no other
reward but to love You more and more.

With a firm love, I will love You with all my heart
while on earth and continue to love
You perfectly during all eternity. Amen.

THE DIVINE SHEPHERD PSALM
(THE 23RD PSALM)

The Lord is my shepherd, I shall not want.
He makes me lie down in green pastures;
He leads me beside still waters; He restores my soul.
He leads me in right paths for His Name's sake.

Even though I walk through the darkest valley,
I fear no evil; for You are with me;
Your rod and Your staff - they comfort me.

You prepare a table before me in
the presence of my enemies;
You anoint my head with oil; my cup overflows.

Surely goodness and mercy shall follow me
all the days of my life, and I shall dwell
in the house of the Lord my whole life long.

DOMINE IESU CHRISTE, REX GLORIAE

O Lord Jesus Christ, King of glory, deliver the souls
of all the faithful departed from the pains of hell
and from the bottomless pit; deliver them out
of the lion's mouth, lest hell should swallow
them up, lest they fall into the outer darkness;
but let Thy standard-bearer Saint Michael bring them
back into Thy holy light, which Thou didst promise
of old to Abraham and to his seed. Amen.

Stained Glass Selected Bibliography

Catechism of the Catholic Church. New York: Doubleday, 1995.

Brown, Sarah and David O'Connor. Glass-Painters. Buffalo: University of Toronto Press, 1991.

Farnsworth, Jean M., Carmen R. Crose, Joseph F. Chorpenning, O.S.F.S., editors. Stained Glass in Catholic Philadelphia. Philadelphia: Saint Joseph's University Press, 2002.

Ferguson, George. Signs & Symbols in Christian Art. New York: Oxford University Press, 1954.

Jamieson, Deborah Stone. Franz Mayer and Company: The Programs of Stained Glass in the Church of the Immaculate Conception, Jacksonville, Florida; and the Sacred Heart Church, Tampa, Florida. Gainesville, FL: The University of Florida Graduate School, 2005.

Metford, JCJ. Dictionary of Christian Lore and Legend. London: Thames and Hudson Ltd., 1983.

Murray, Peter and Linda. Oxford Dictionary of Christian Art. New York: Oxford University Press, 2004.

Raguin, Virginia Chieffo. Stained Glass from its Origins to the Present. New York: Harry N. Abrams, Inc., 2003.

_____. "John A. Riordan: SGAA Life Member," Stained Glass 81 (Spring 1986): 21-24

Schiller, Gertrude. Iconography of Christen Art, v. 1. Greenwich, CT: New York Graphic Society, Ltd., 1971.

Sill, Gertrude Grace. A Handbook of Symbols in Christian Art. New York: Macmillan Publishing Co., Inc., 1975.